Build It!

Make Supercool Models with Your Favorite LEGO® Parts

THINGS THAT FLOAT

Jennifer Kemmeter

GRAPHIC ARTS
BOOKS®

Contents

Sailboats

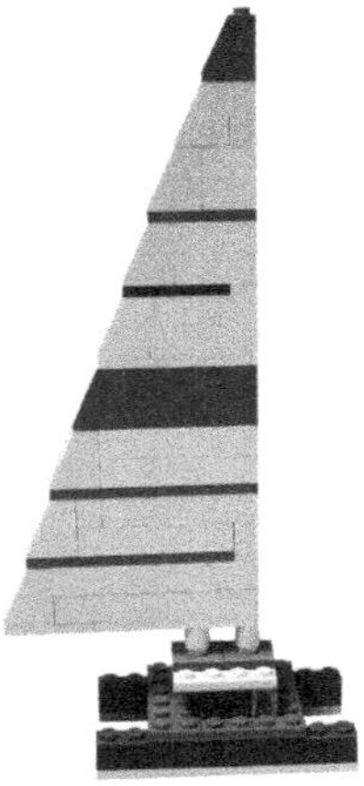

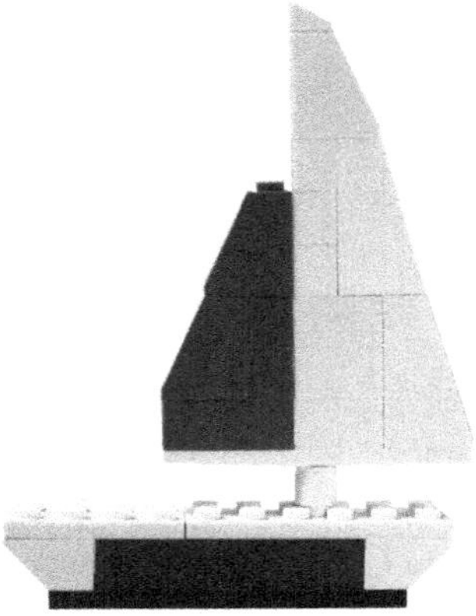

Sports Boats

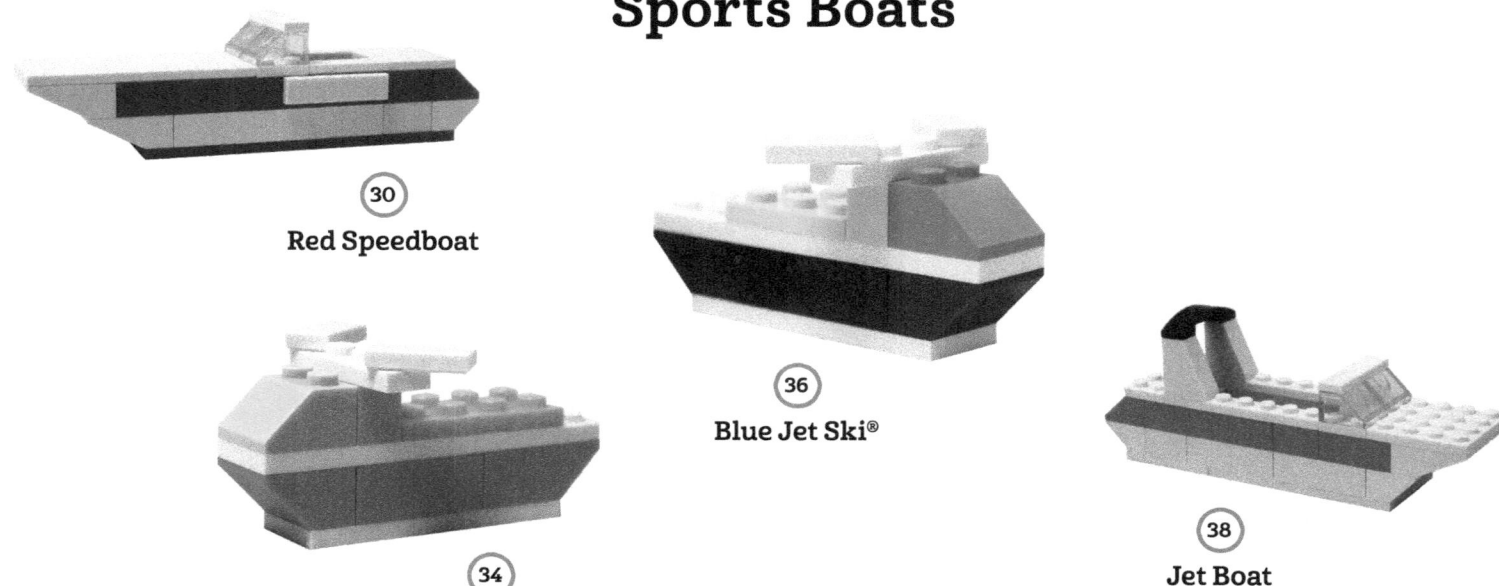

Boat-a-palooza

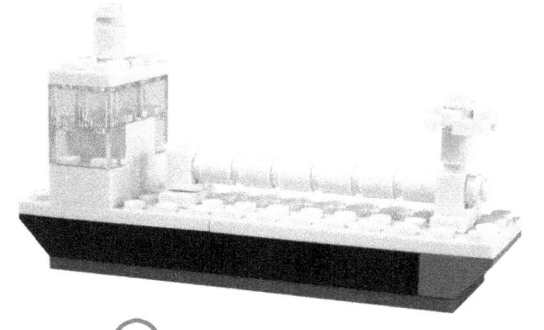

44

Oil Tanker

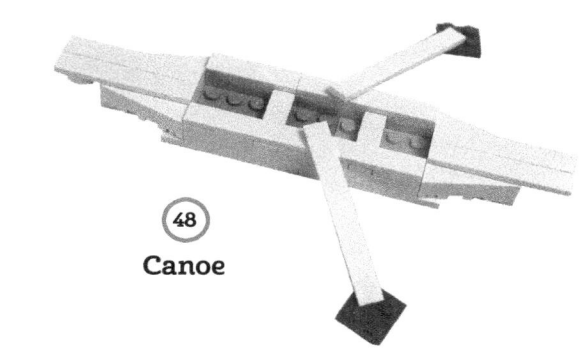

48

Canoe

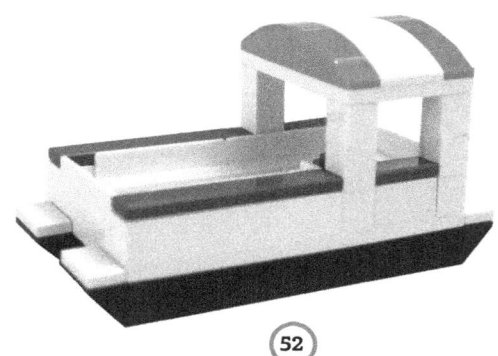

52

Pontoon

57

Kayak

60

Trimaran

68

Super Yacht

How to Use This Book

What you will be building.

Build an Orange Sailboat

A photo of what your finished sailboat will look like.

An illustration of the finished sailboat that looks like the pictures in the steps.

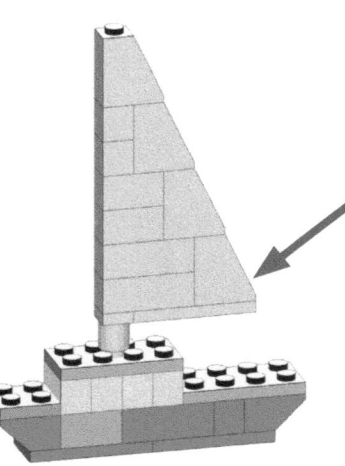

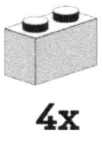
4x

1x

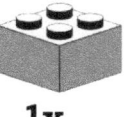
1x

1x

2x

1x

2x

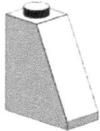
2x

2x

1x

1x

2x

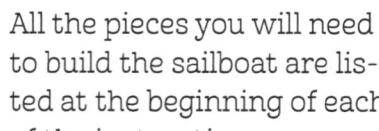
4x

All the pieces you will need to build the sailboat are listed at the beginning of each of the instructions.

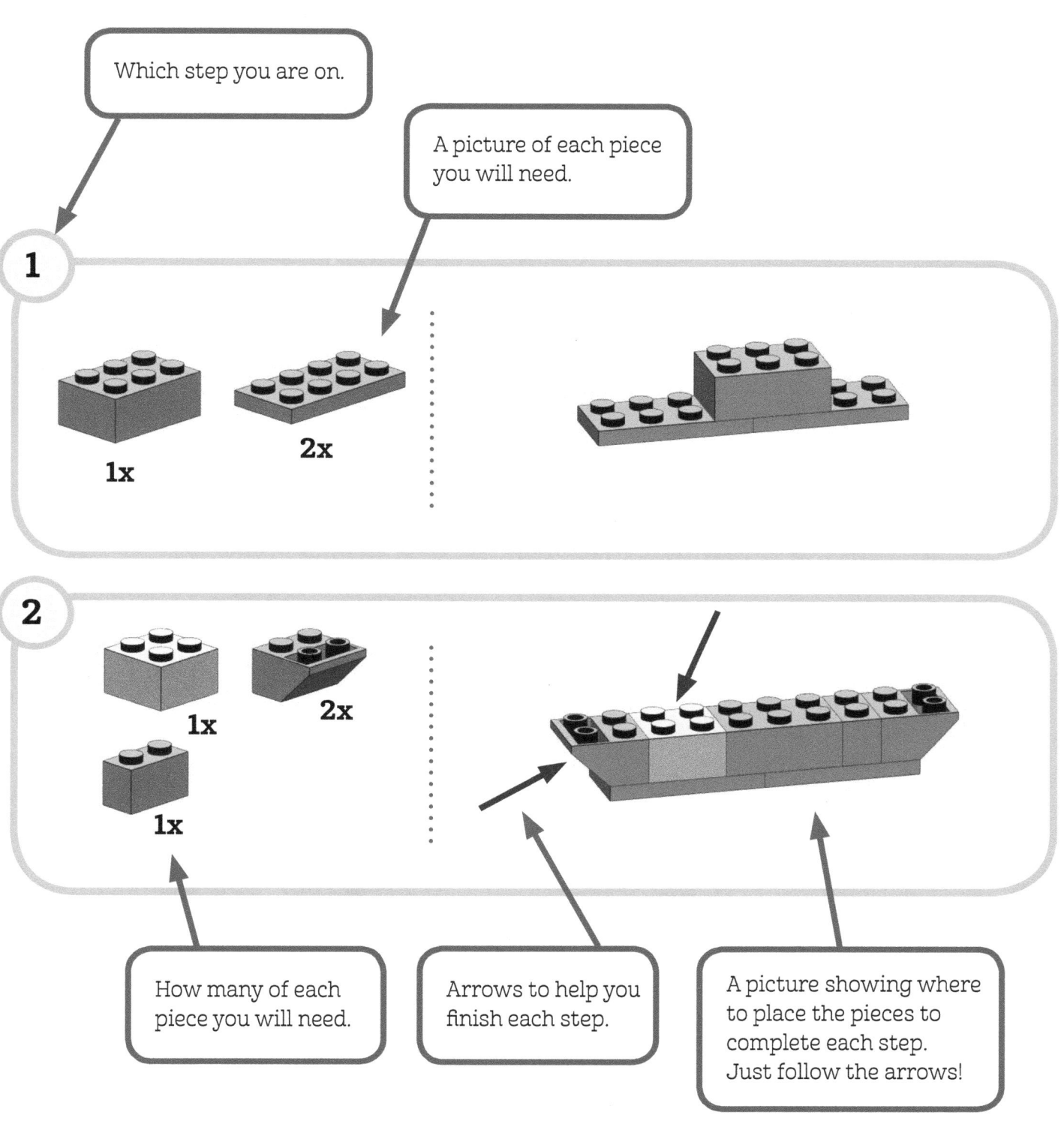

Sailboats

Orange Sailboat

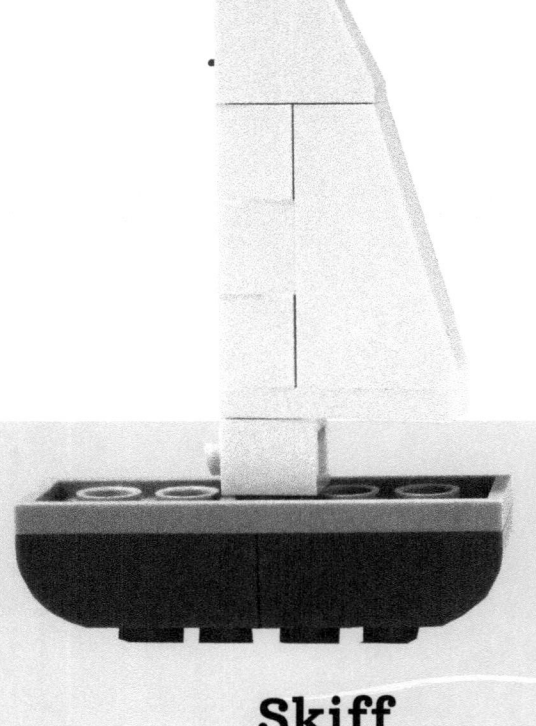

Skiff

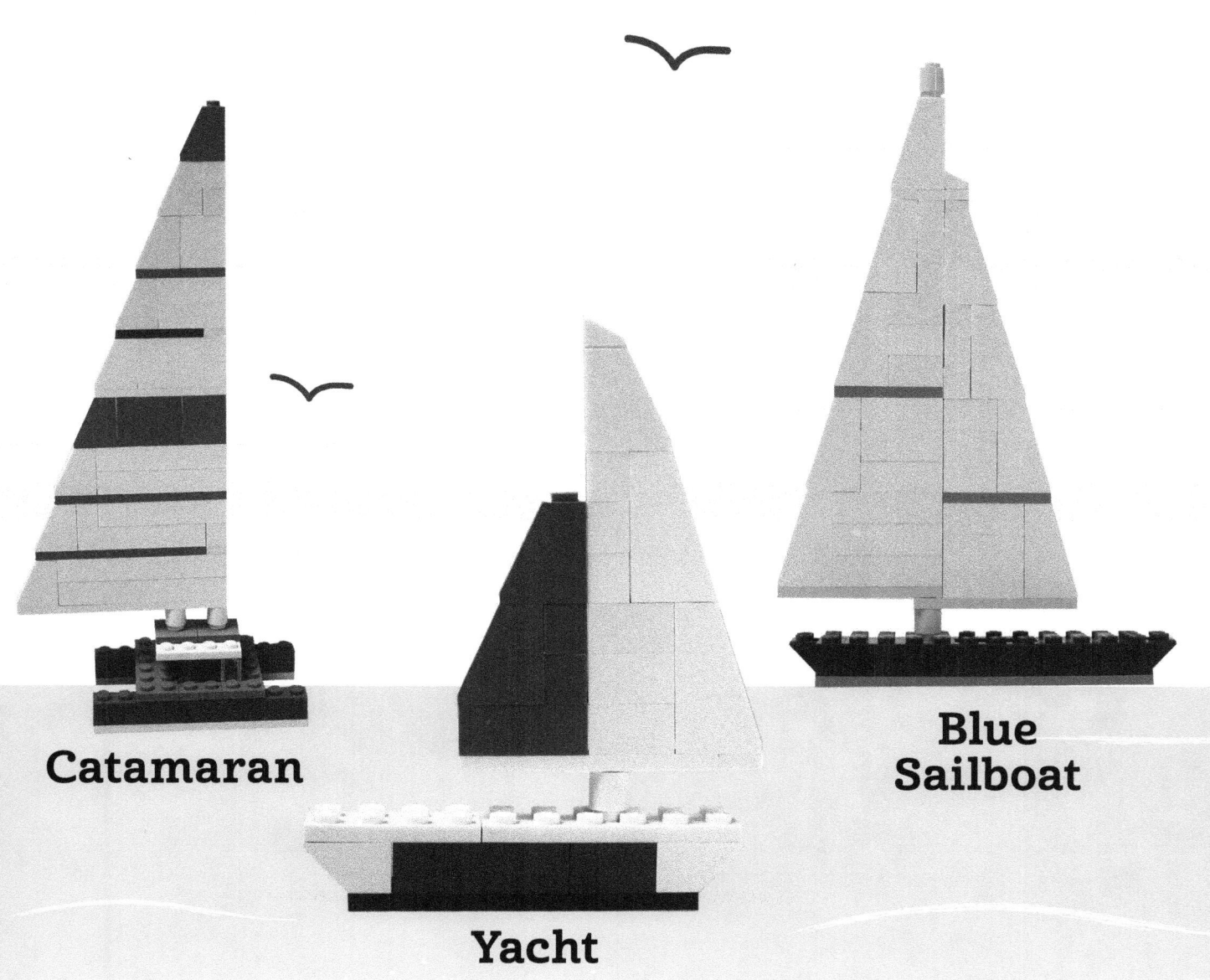

Catamaran

Yacht

Blue Sailboat

Build an Orange Sailboat

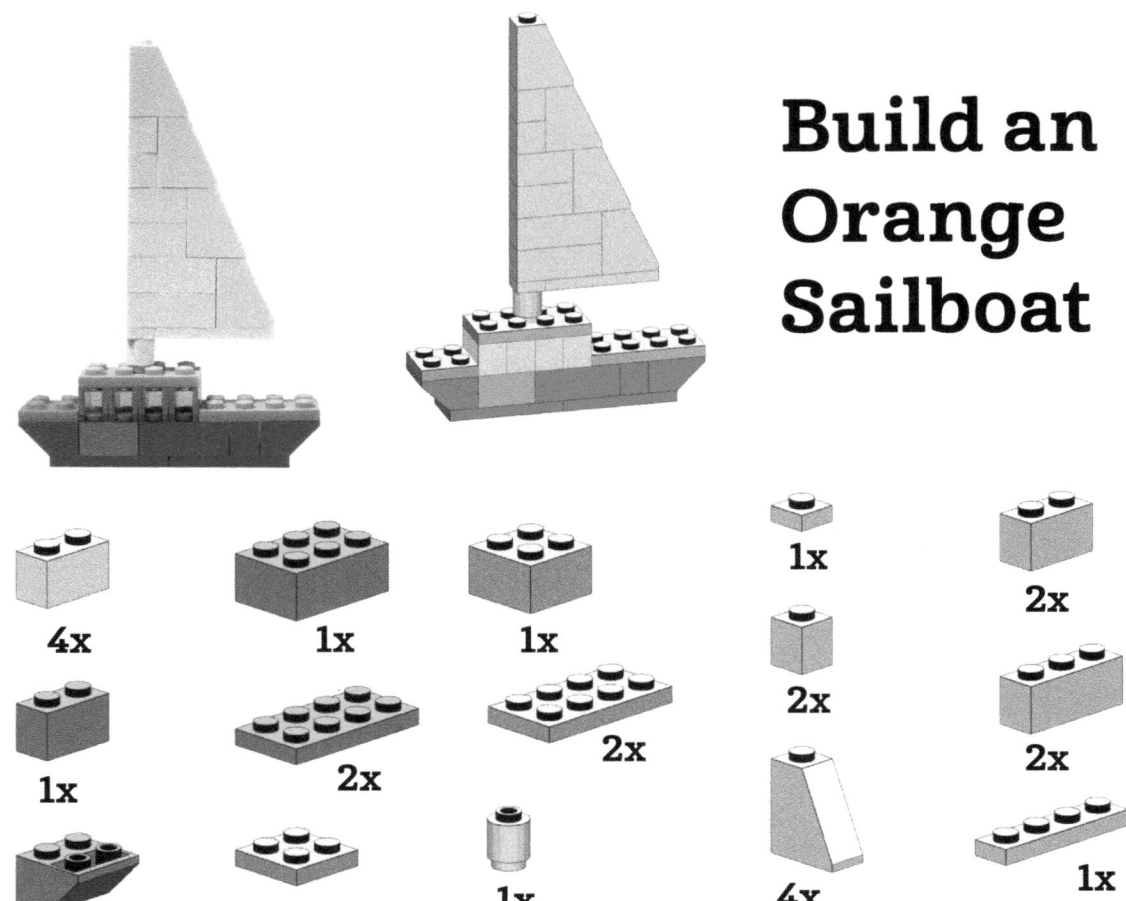

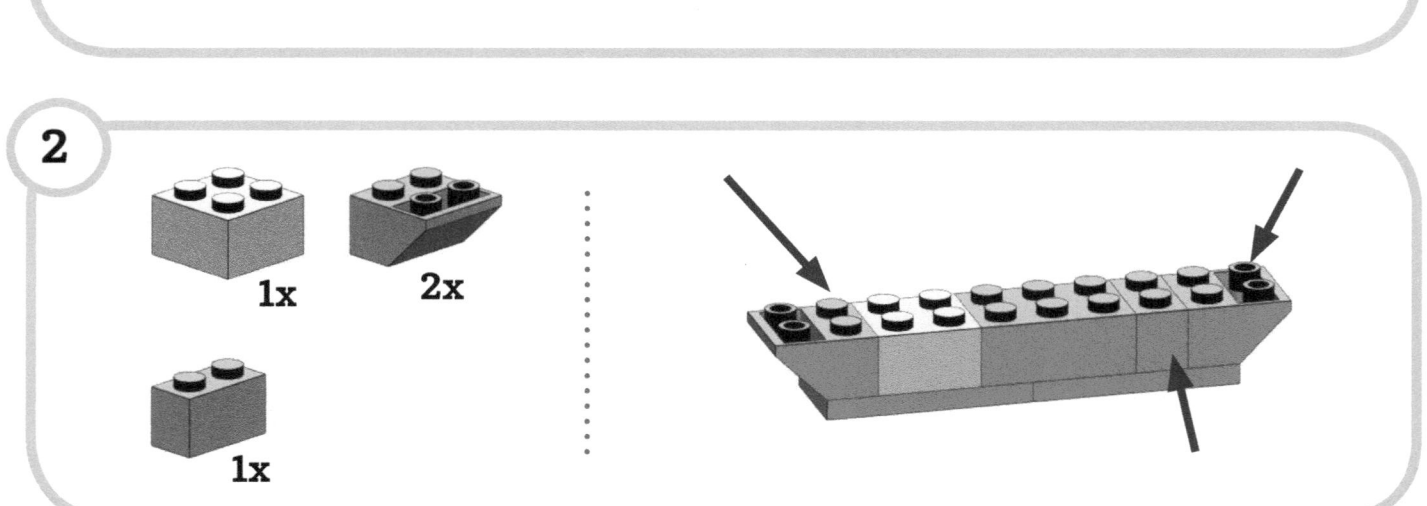

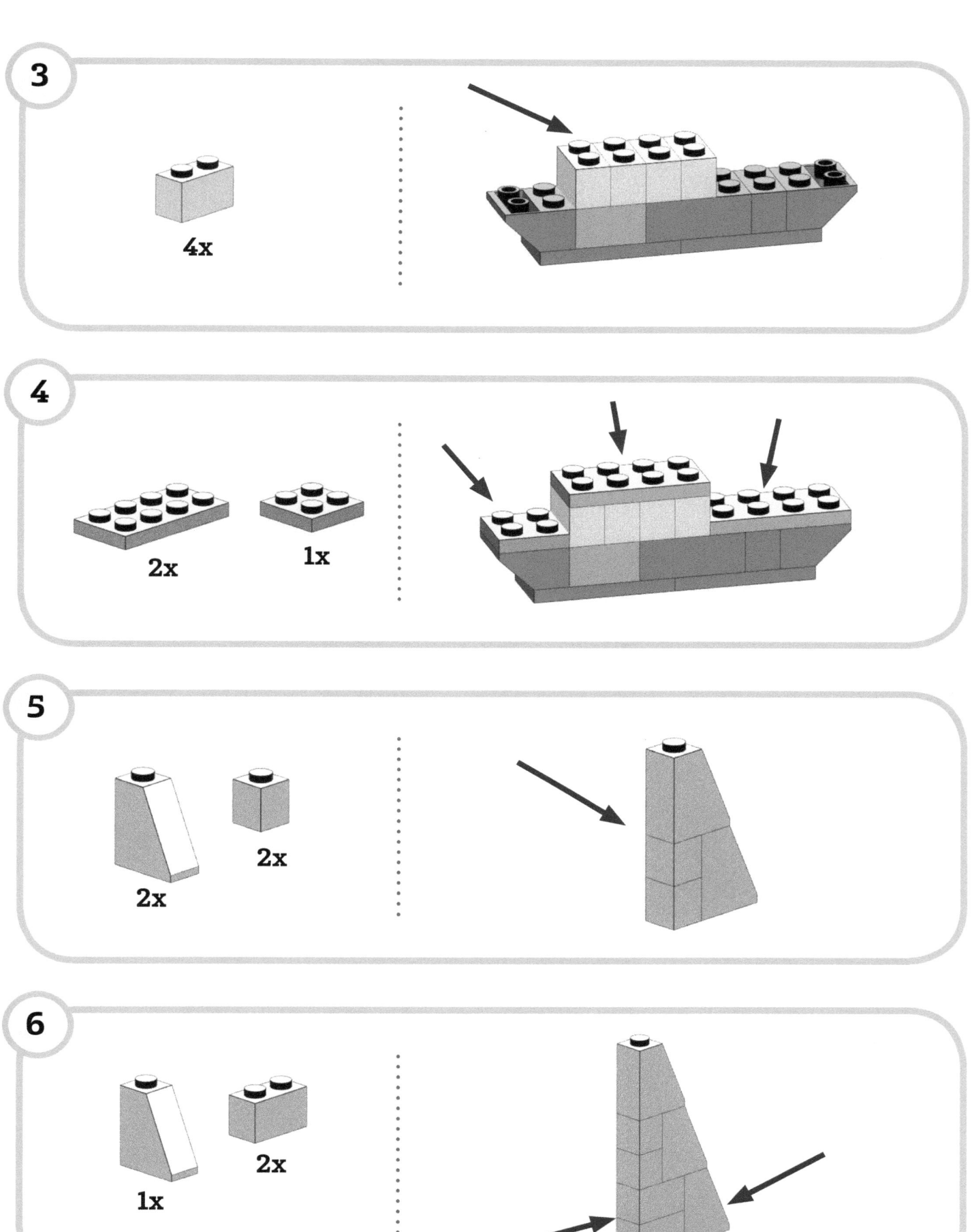

3 4x

4 2x 1x

5 2x 2x

6 1x 2x

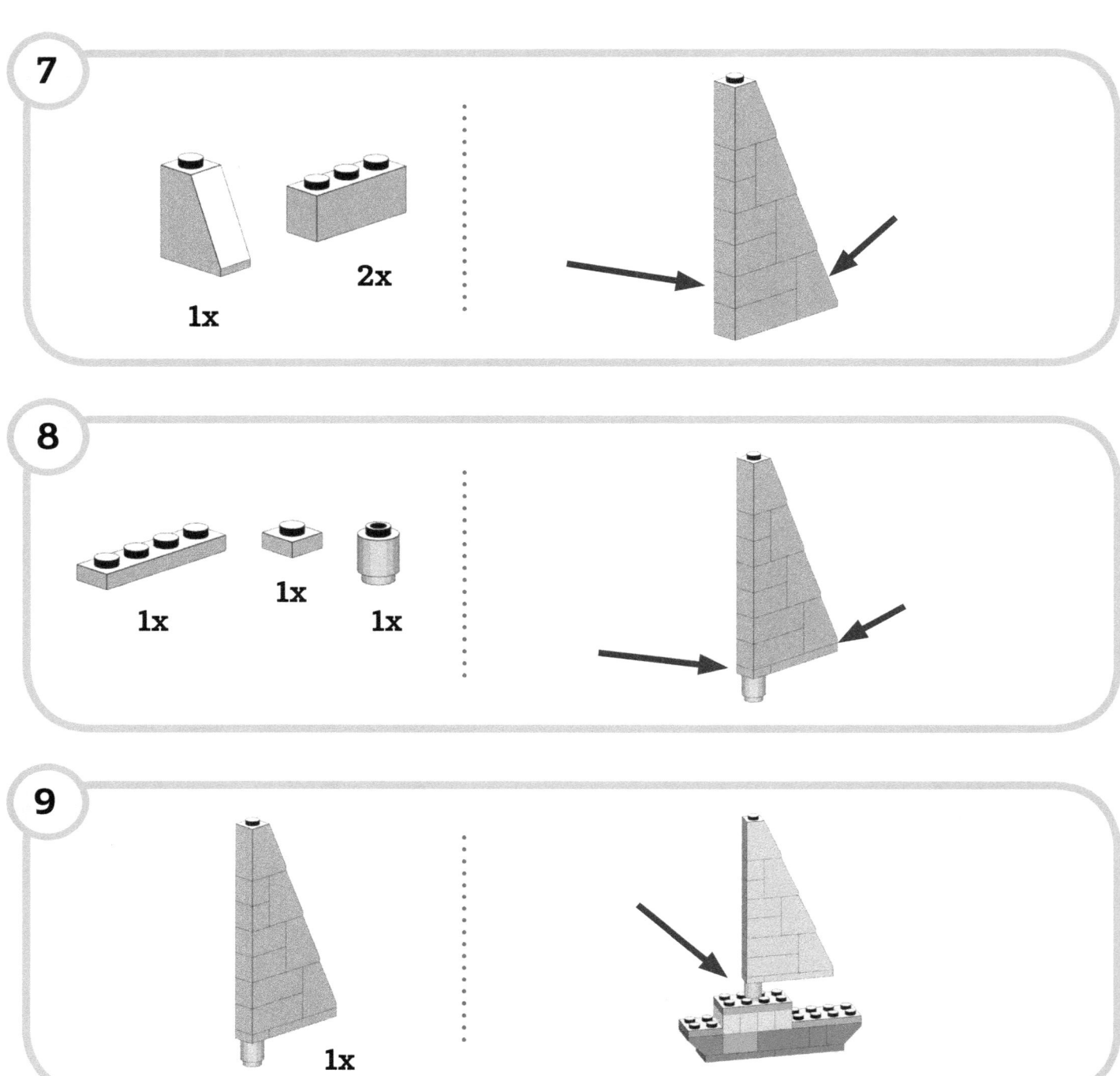

7 1x 2x

8 1x 1x 1x

9 1x

Build a Skiff

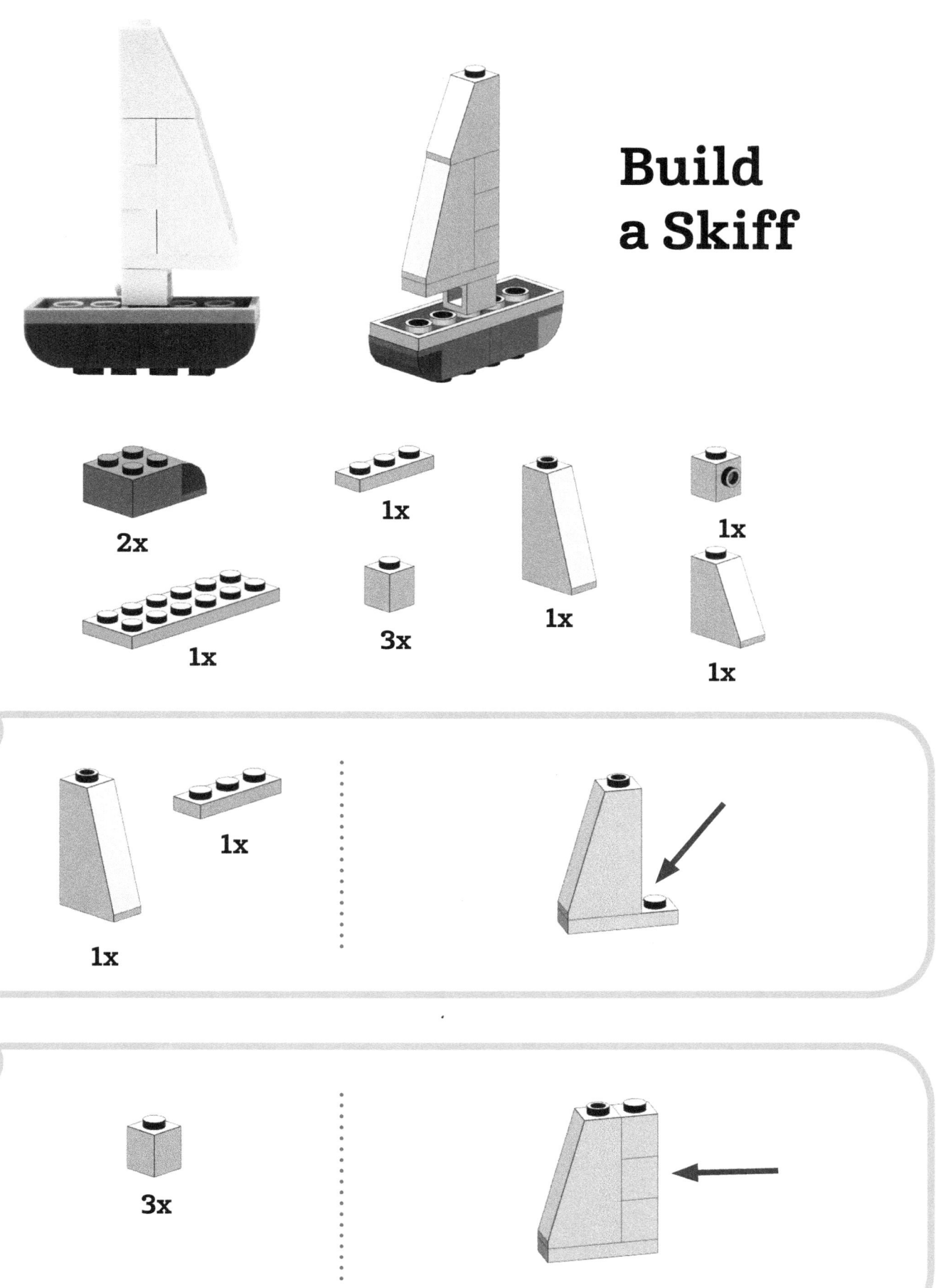

1

2

3

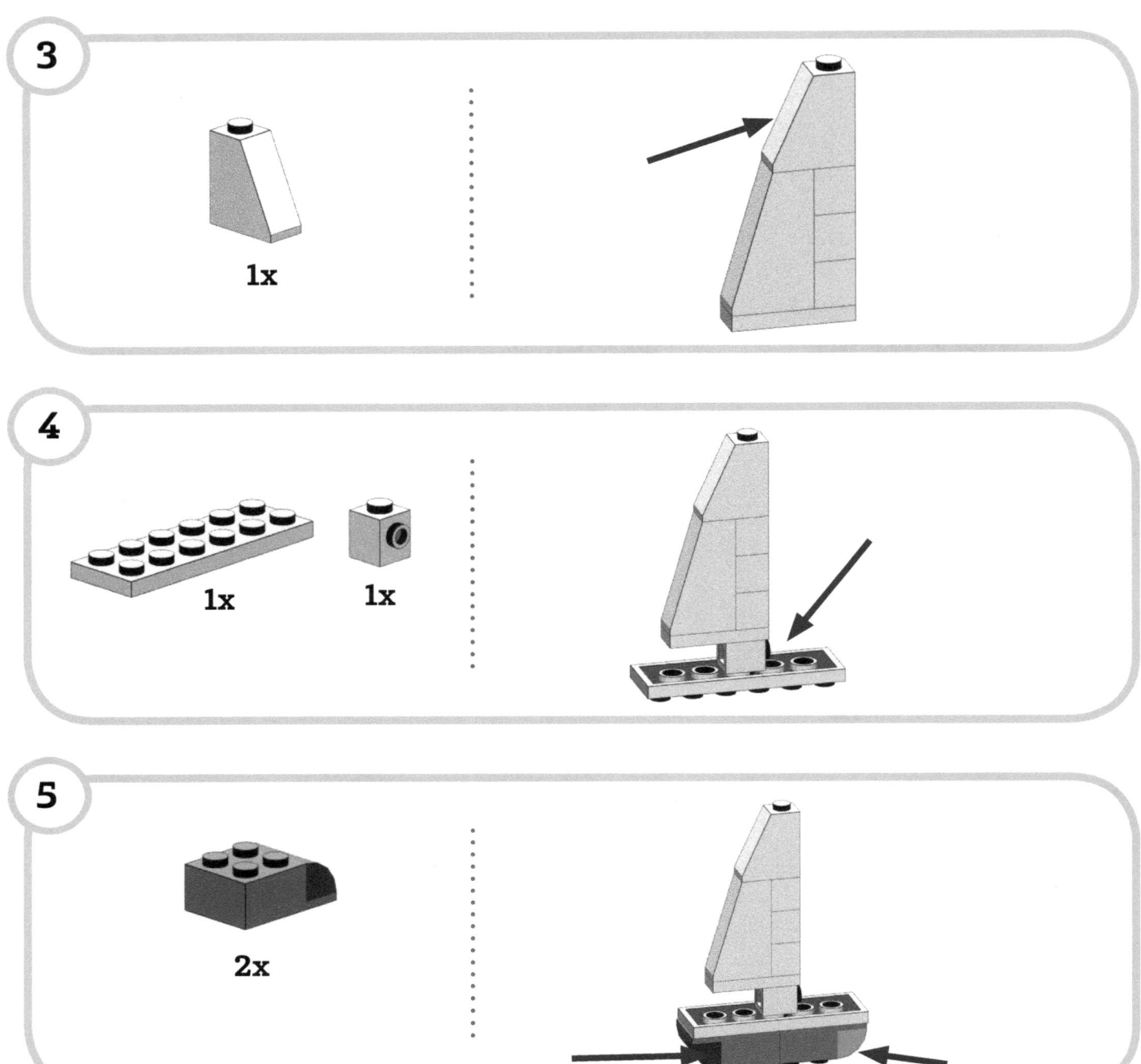

1x

4

1x 1x

5

2x

Build a Catamaran

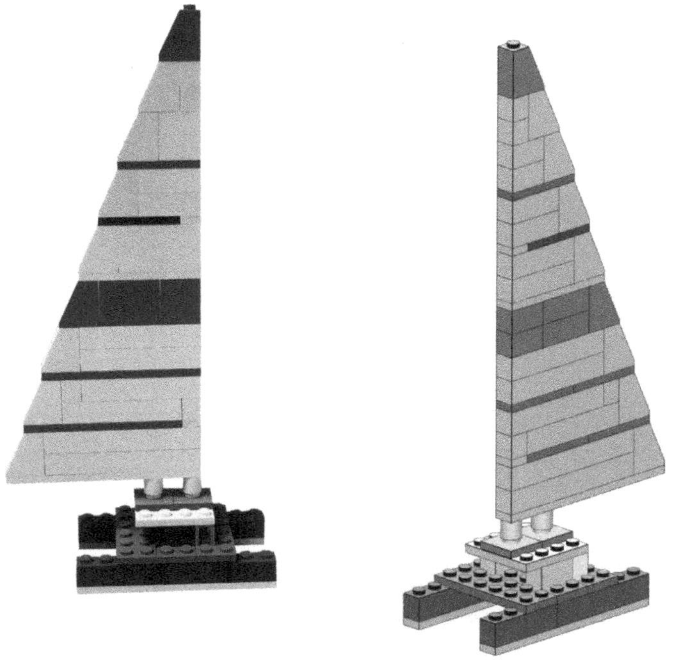

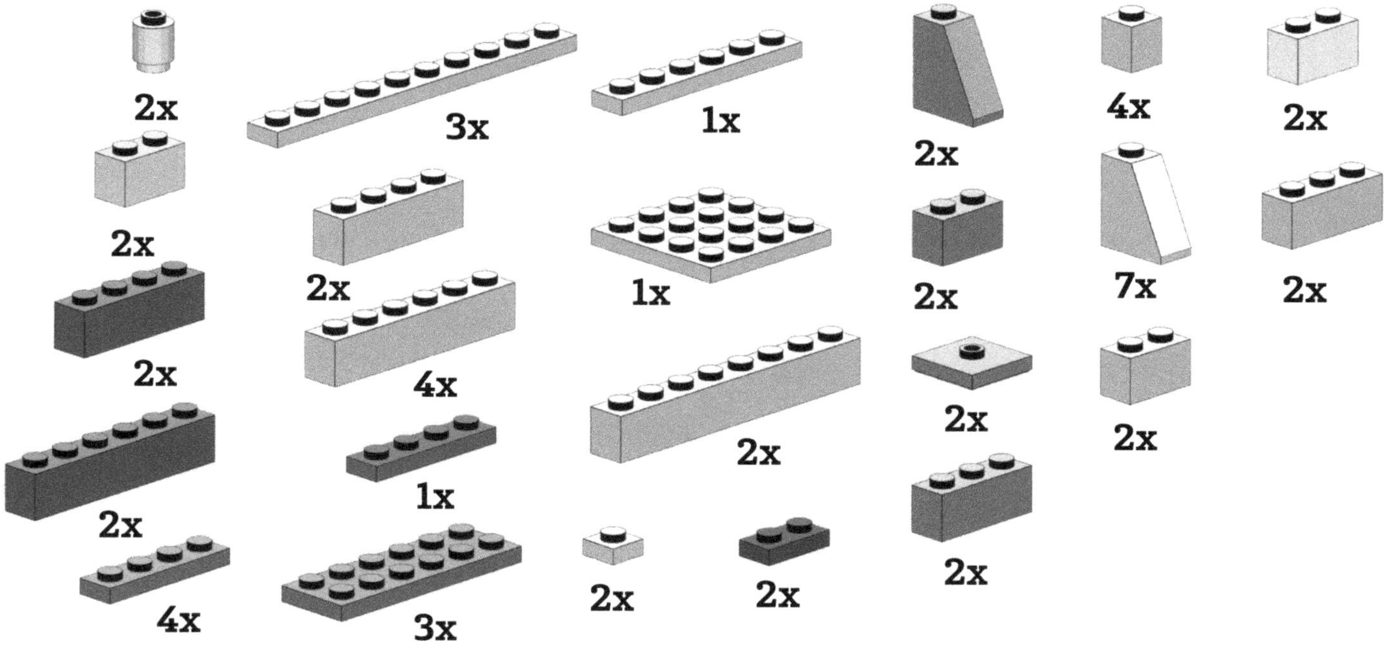

2x

3x

1x

2x

4x

2x

2x

2x

2x

1x

2x

2x

7x

2x

2x

4x

2x

1x

2x

2x

2x

2x

4x

3x

2x

2x

2x

1

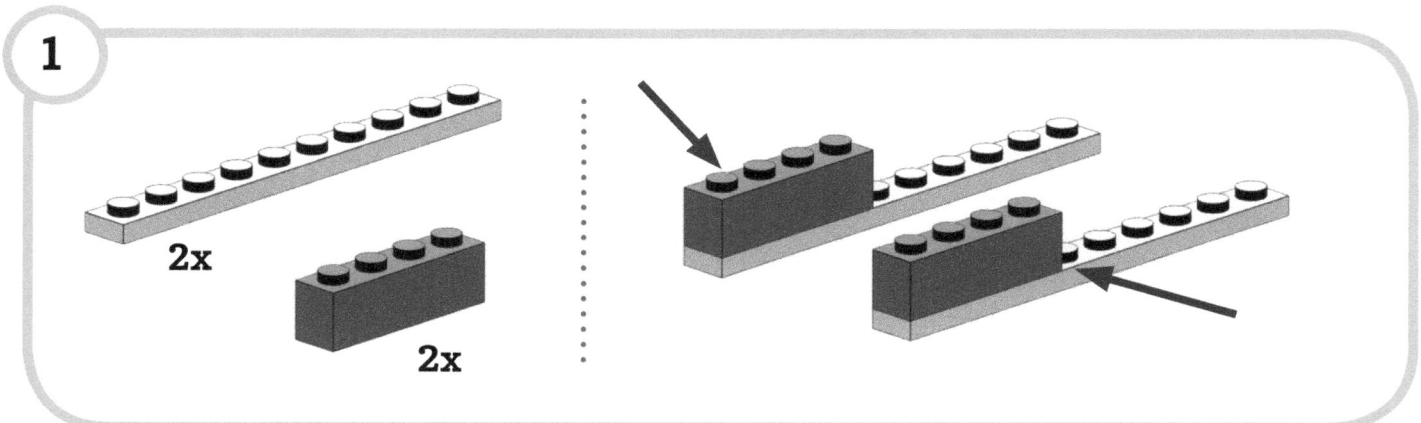

2x

2x

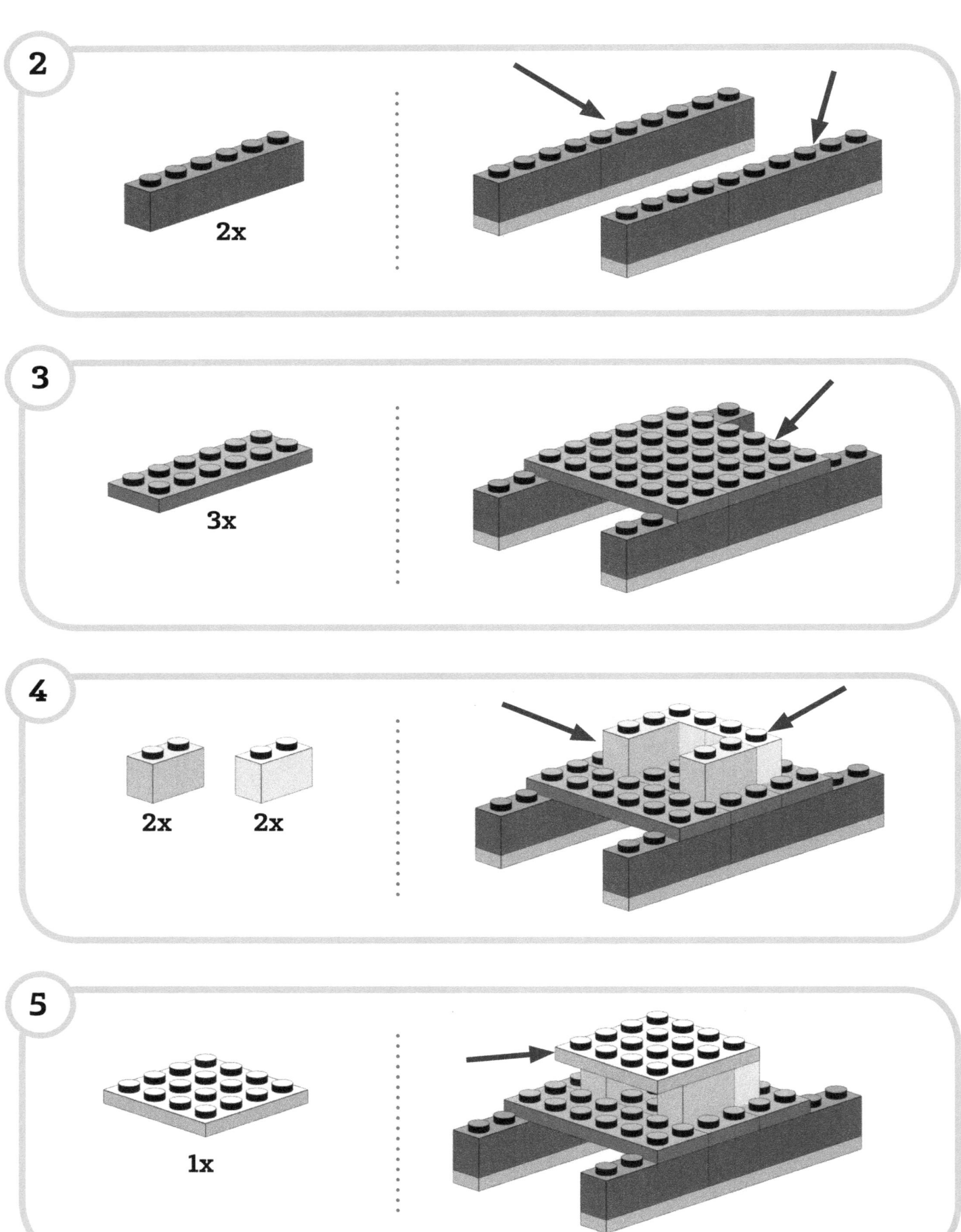

2 2x

3 3x

4 2x 2x

5 1x

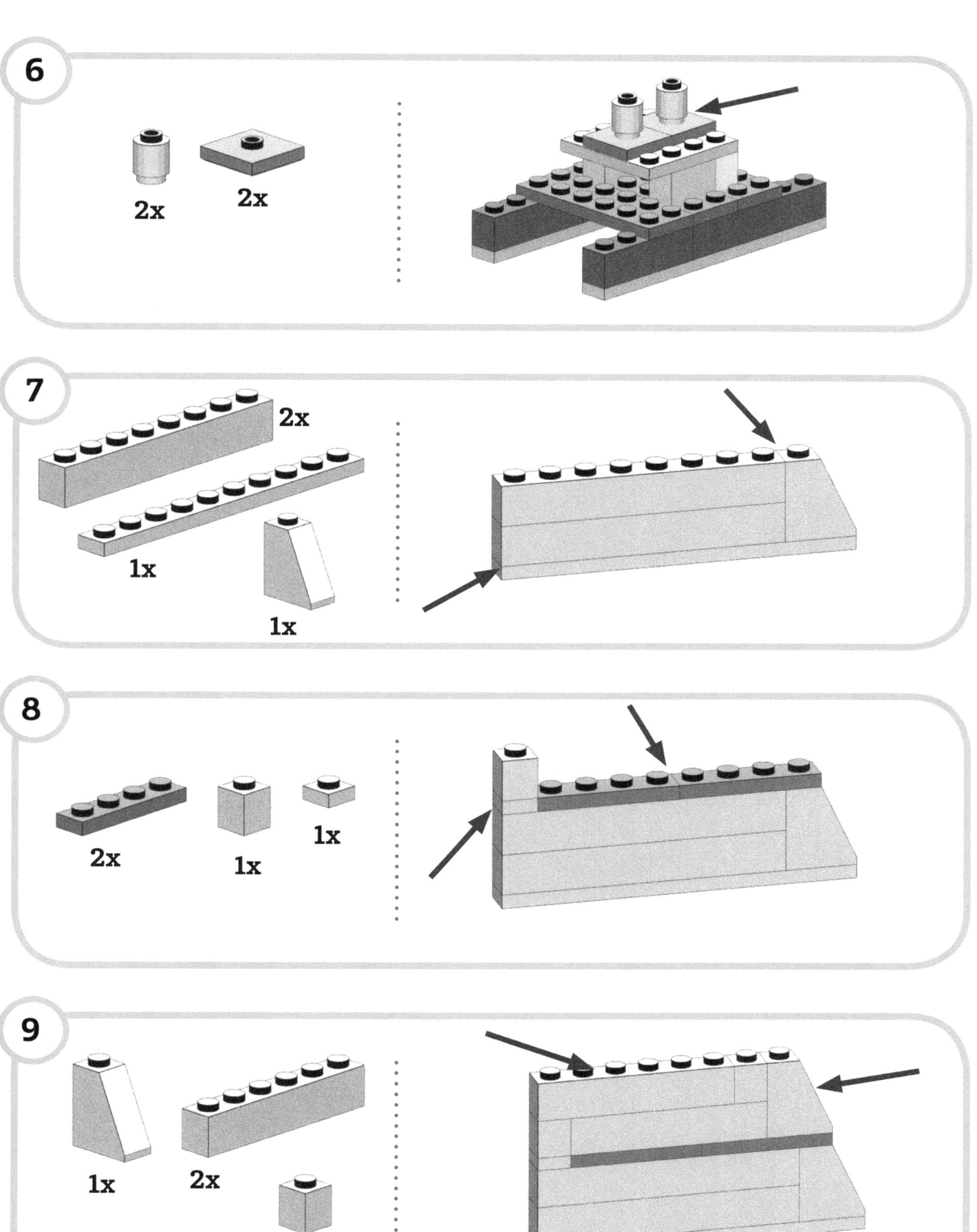

10

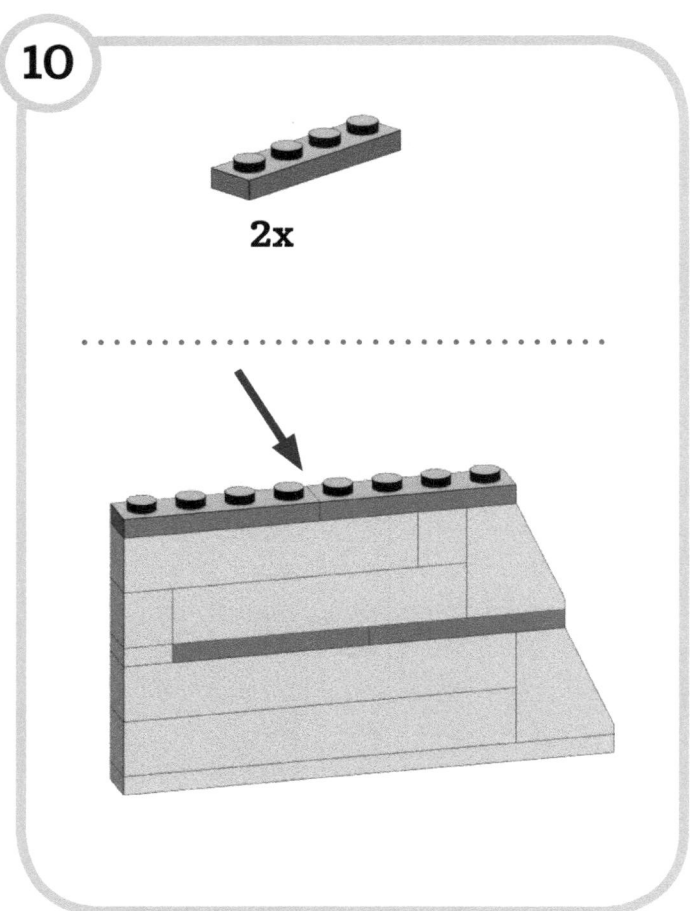

2x

11

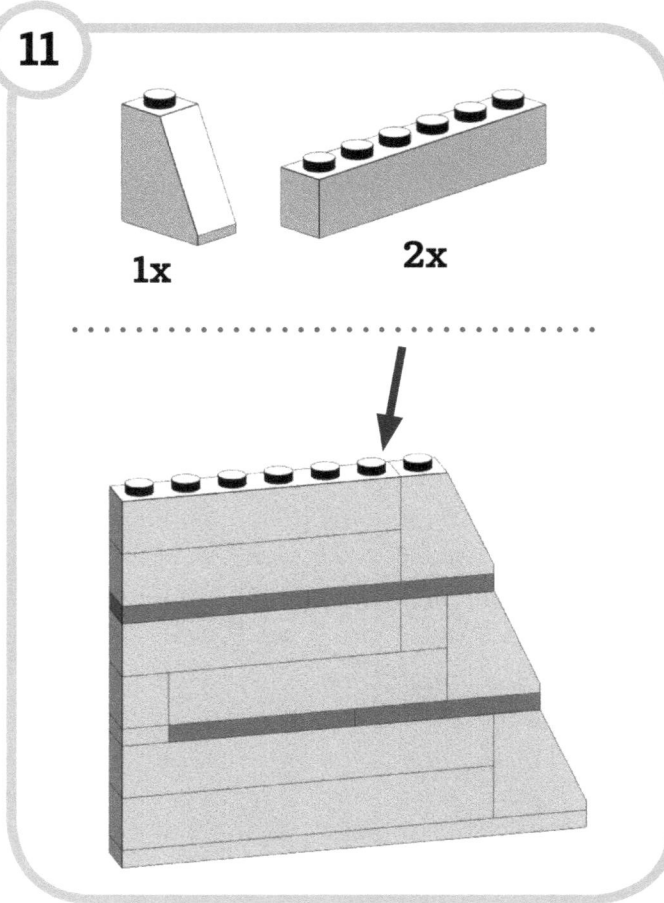

1x   2x

12

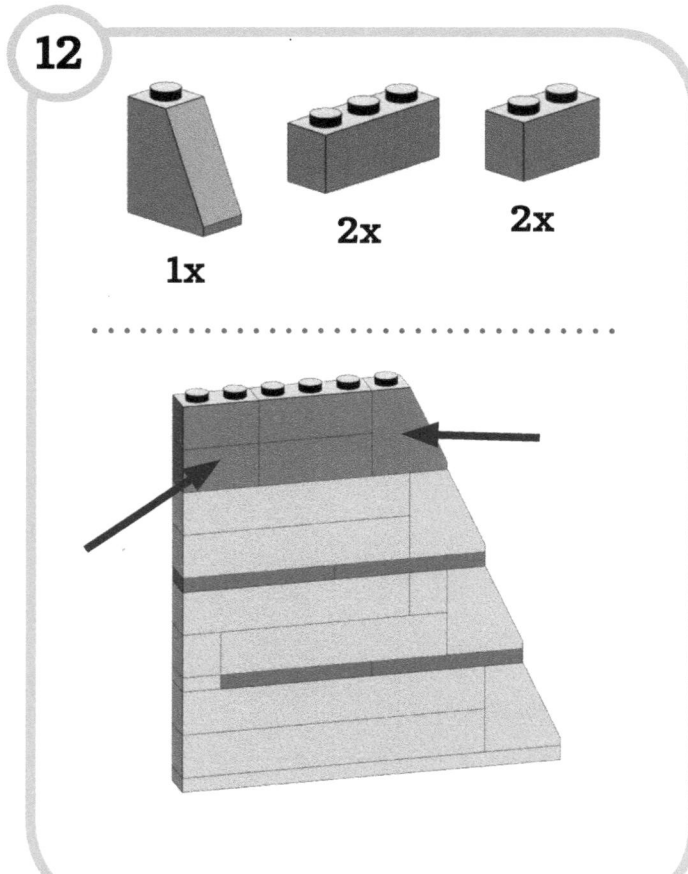

1x   2x   2x

13

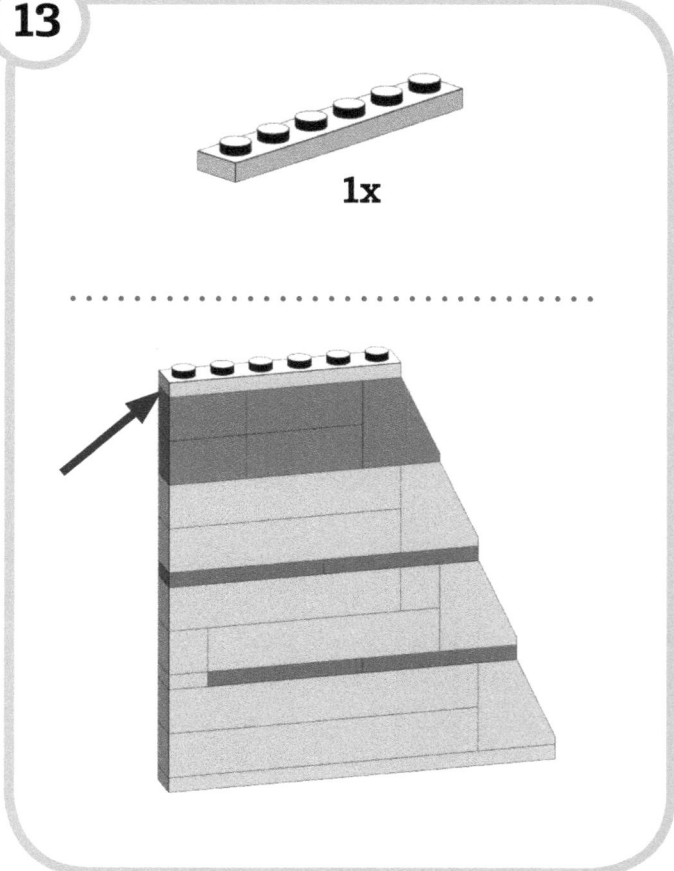

1x

14

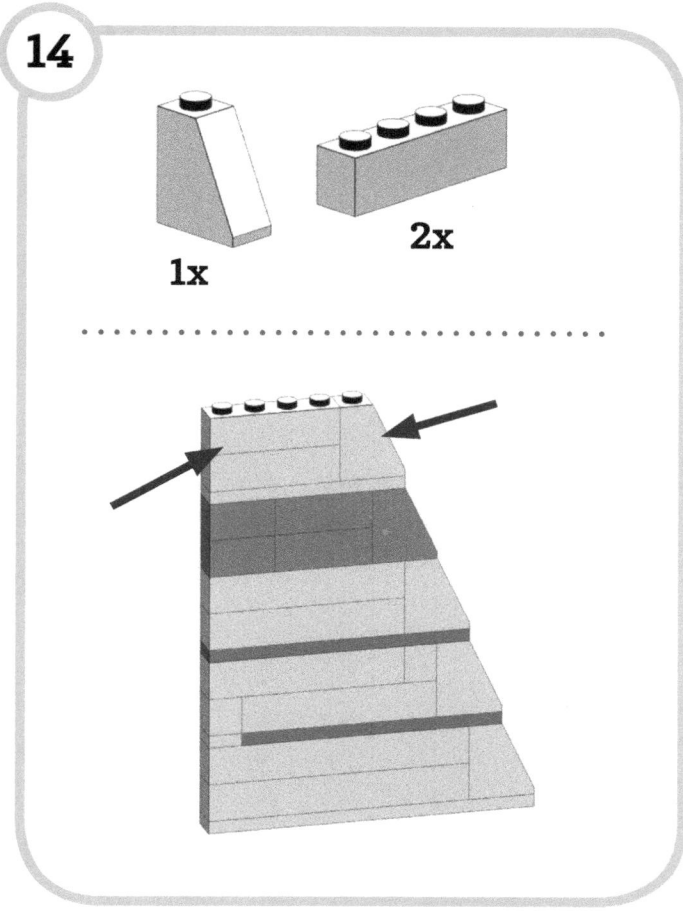

1x 2x

15

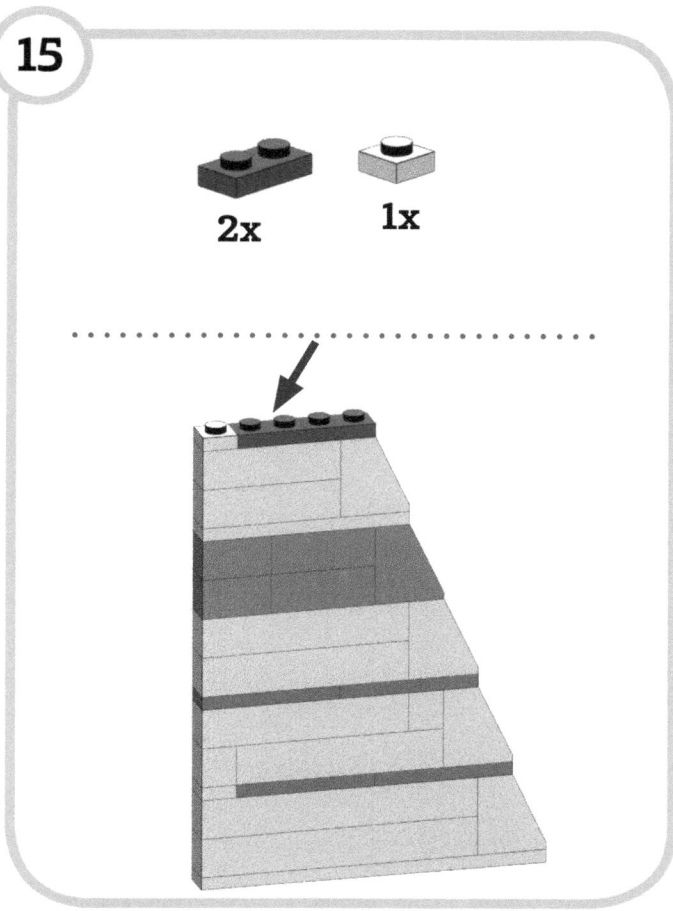

2x 1x

16

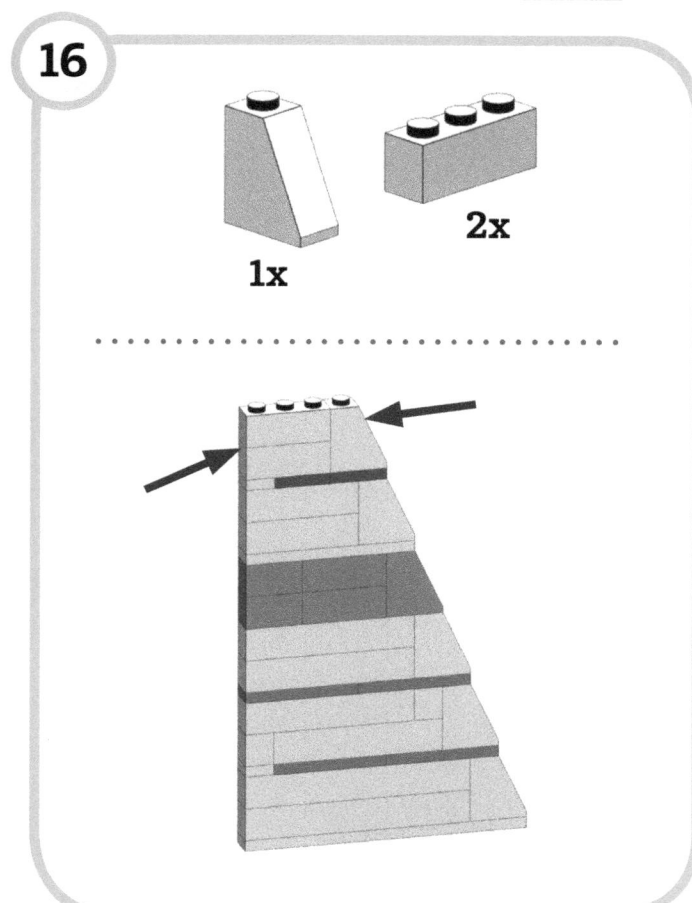

1x 2x

17

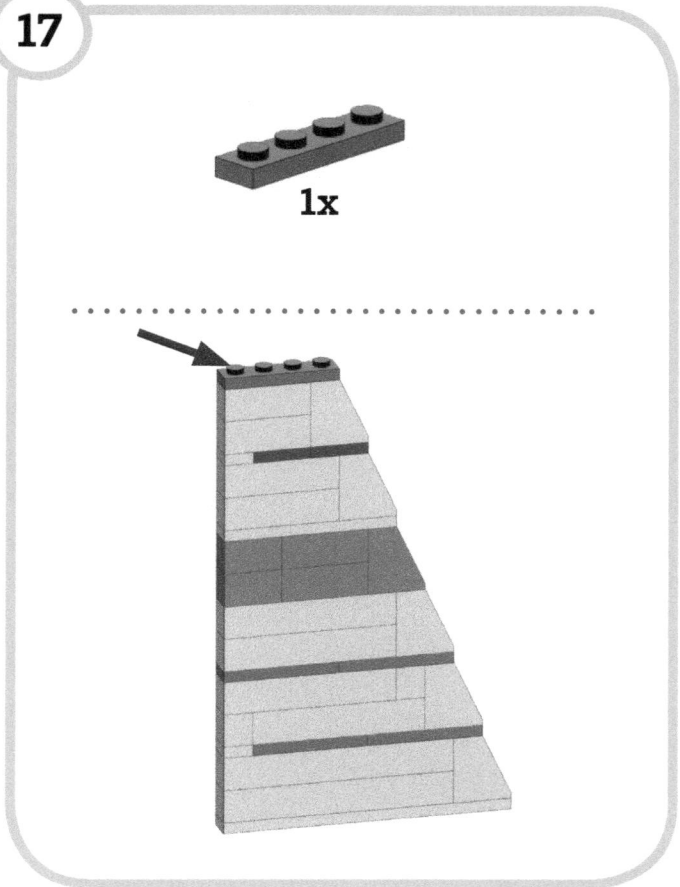

1x

18

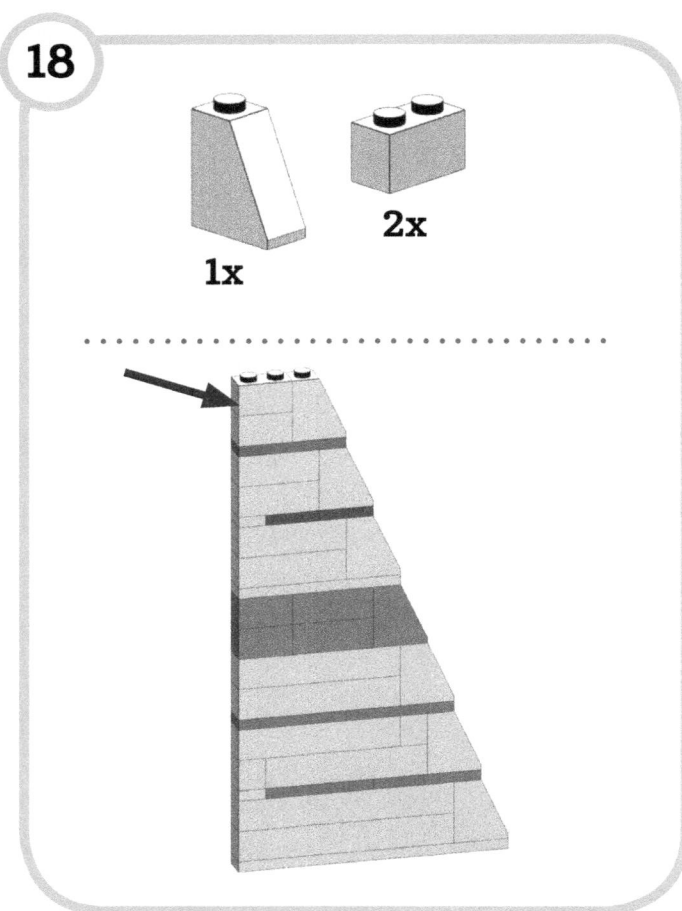

1x 2x

19

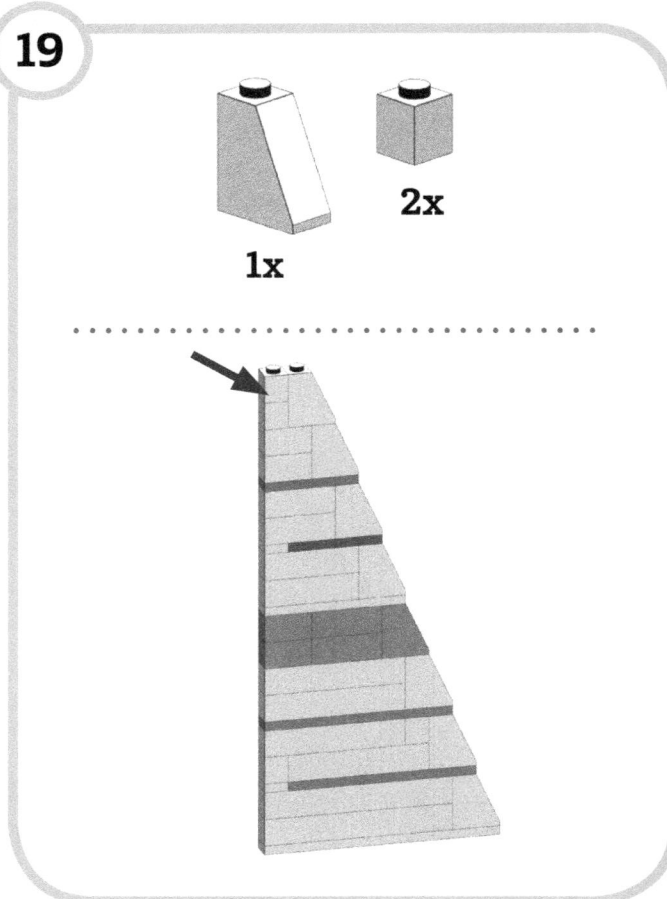

1x 2x

20

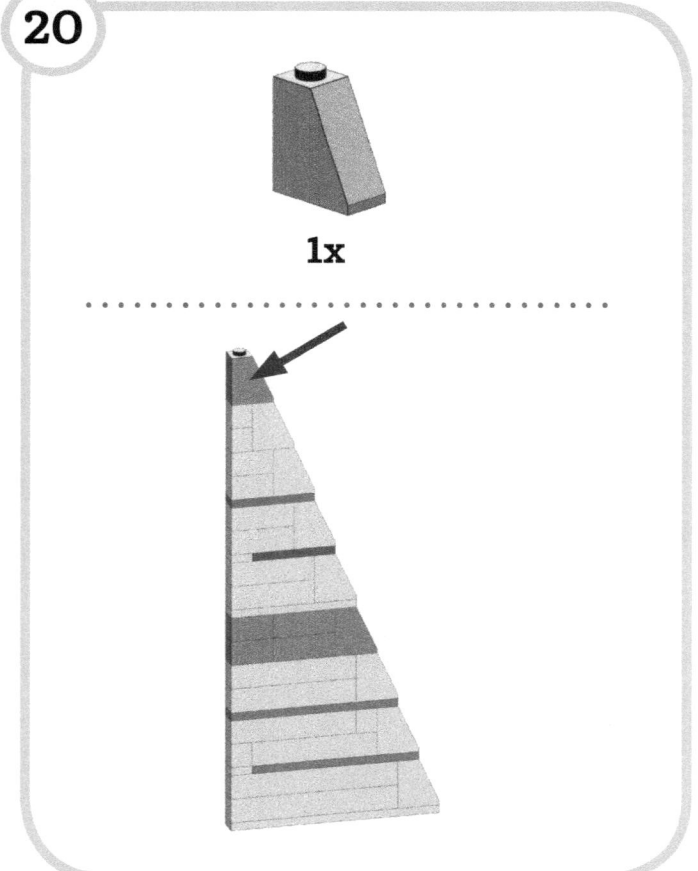

1x

21

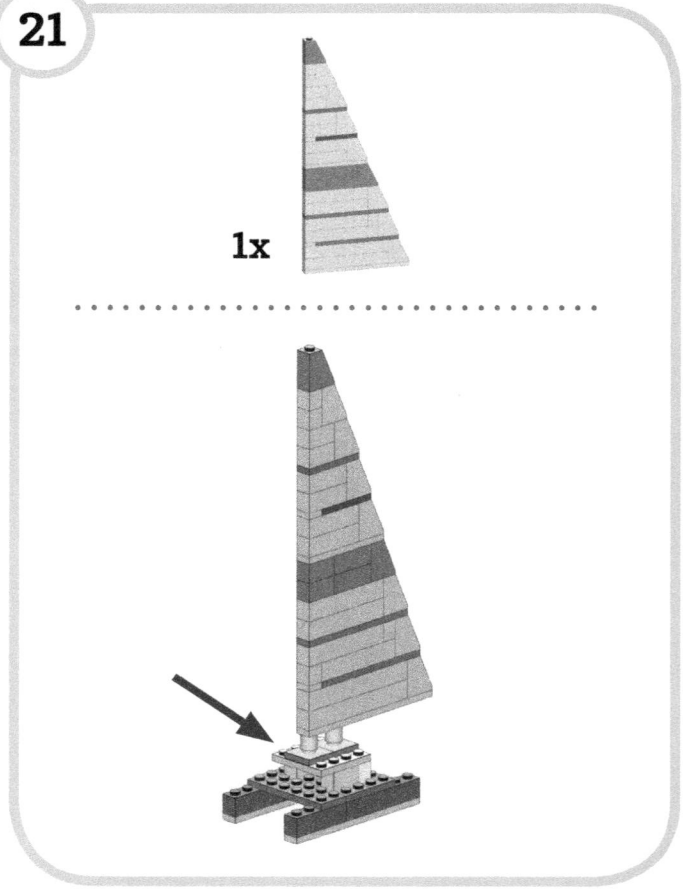

1x

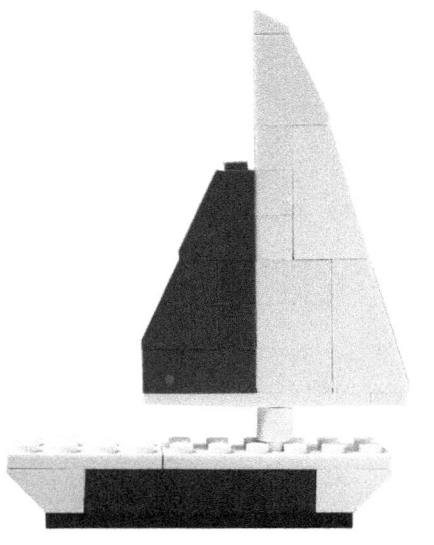
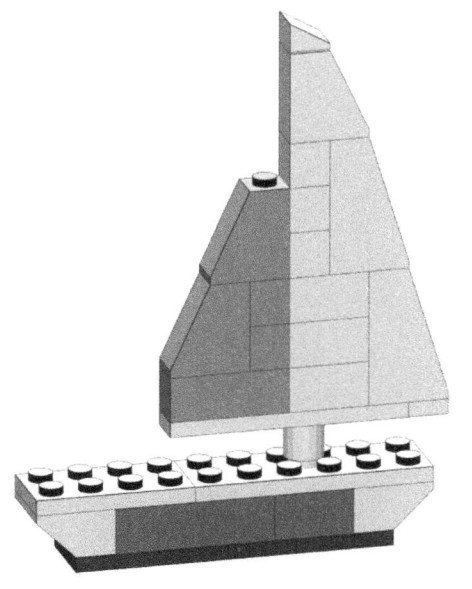

Build
a Yacht

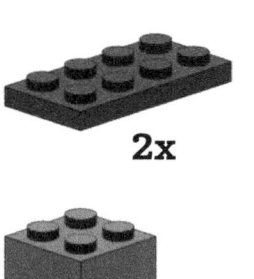
2x

1x

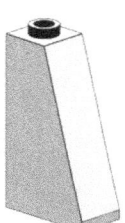
2x

2x

1x

1x

3x

2x

1x

1x

3x

1x

1x

1x

2x

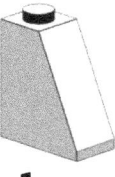
1x

1x

1

1x   2x

19

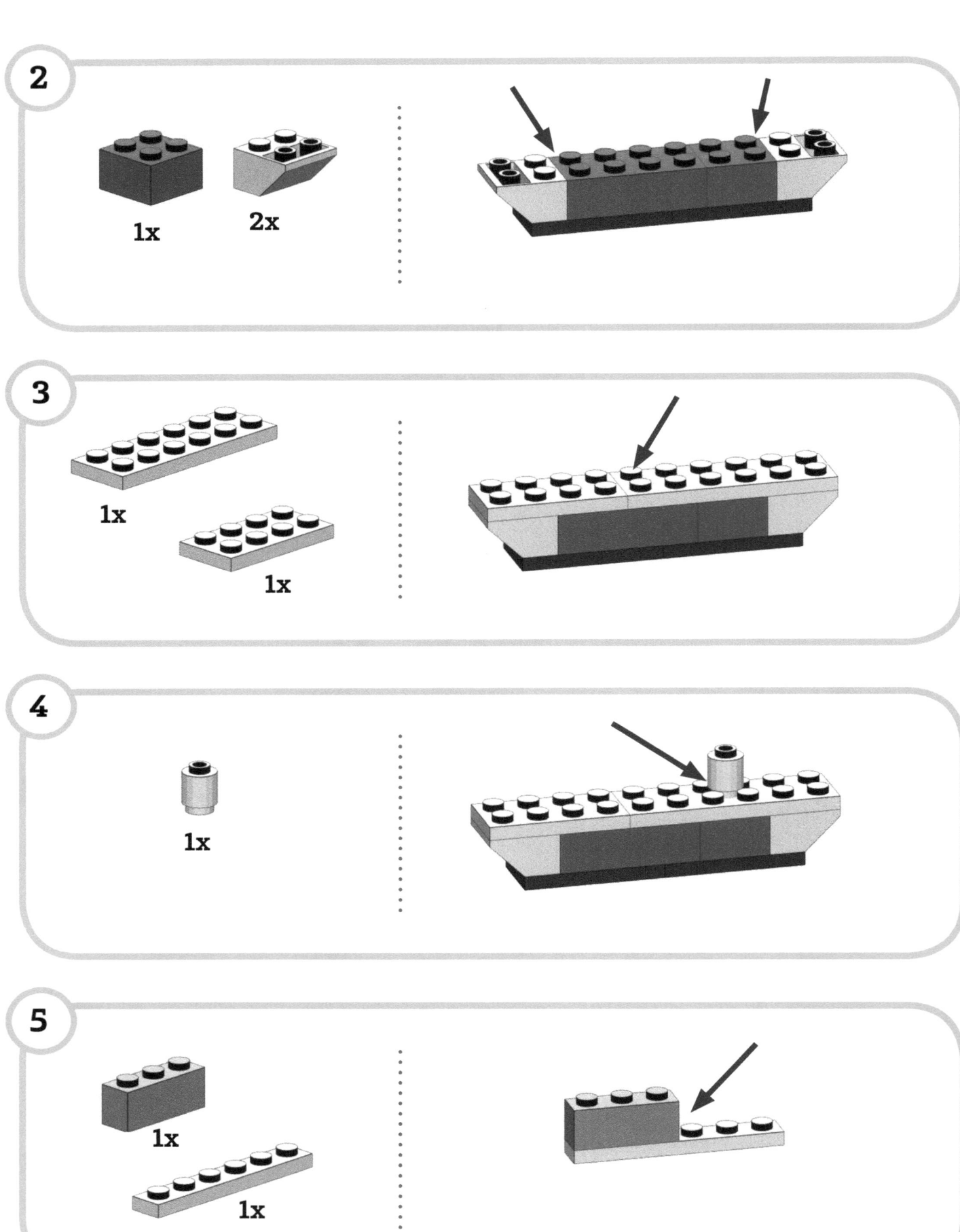

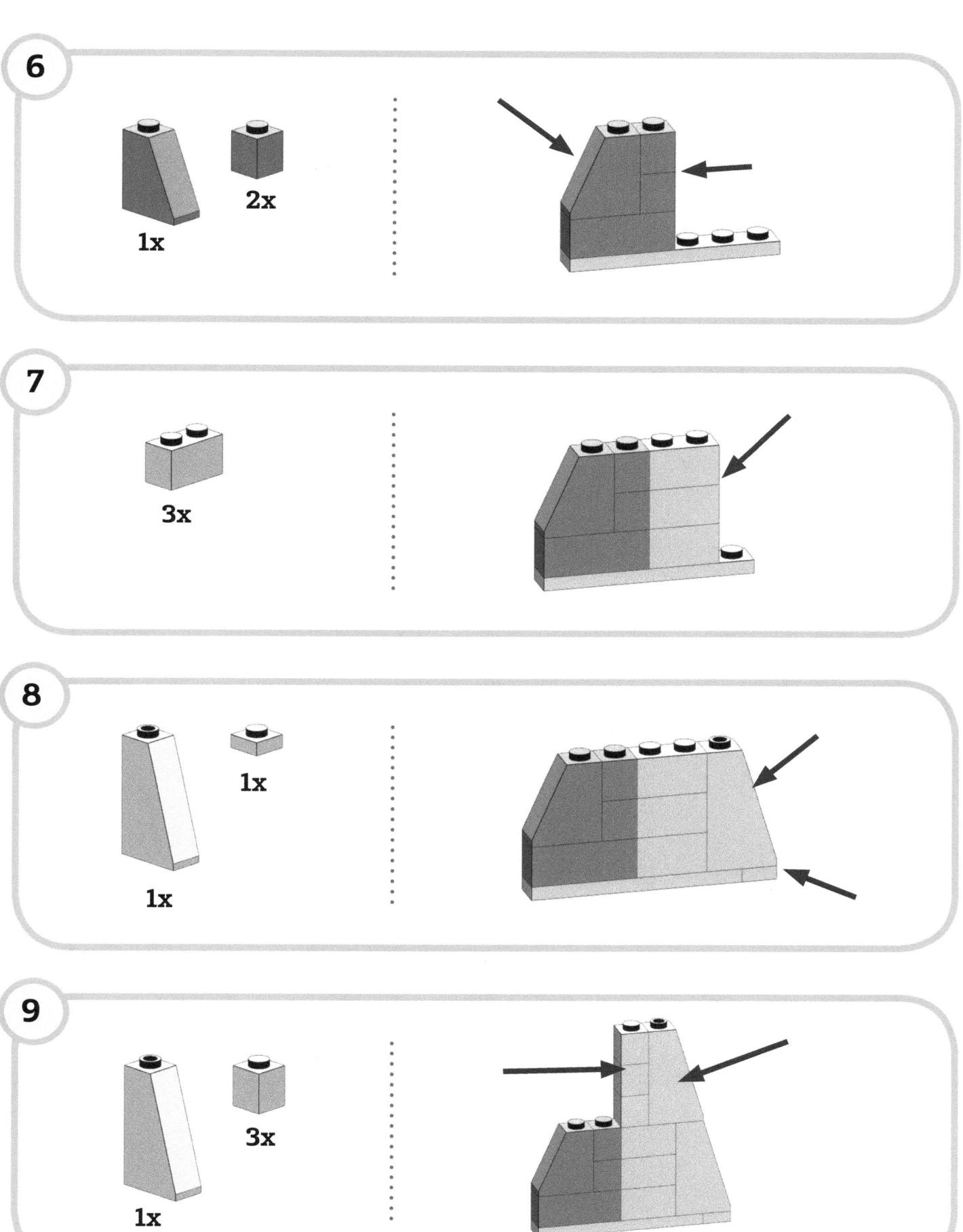

6

1x 2x

7

3x

8

1x 1x

9

1x 3x

10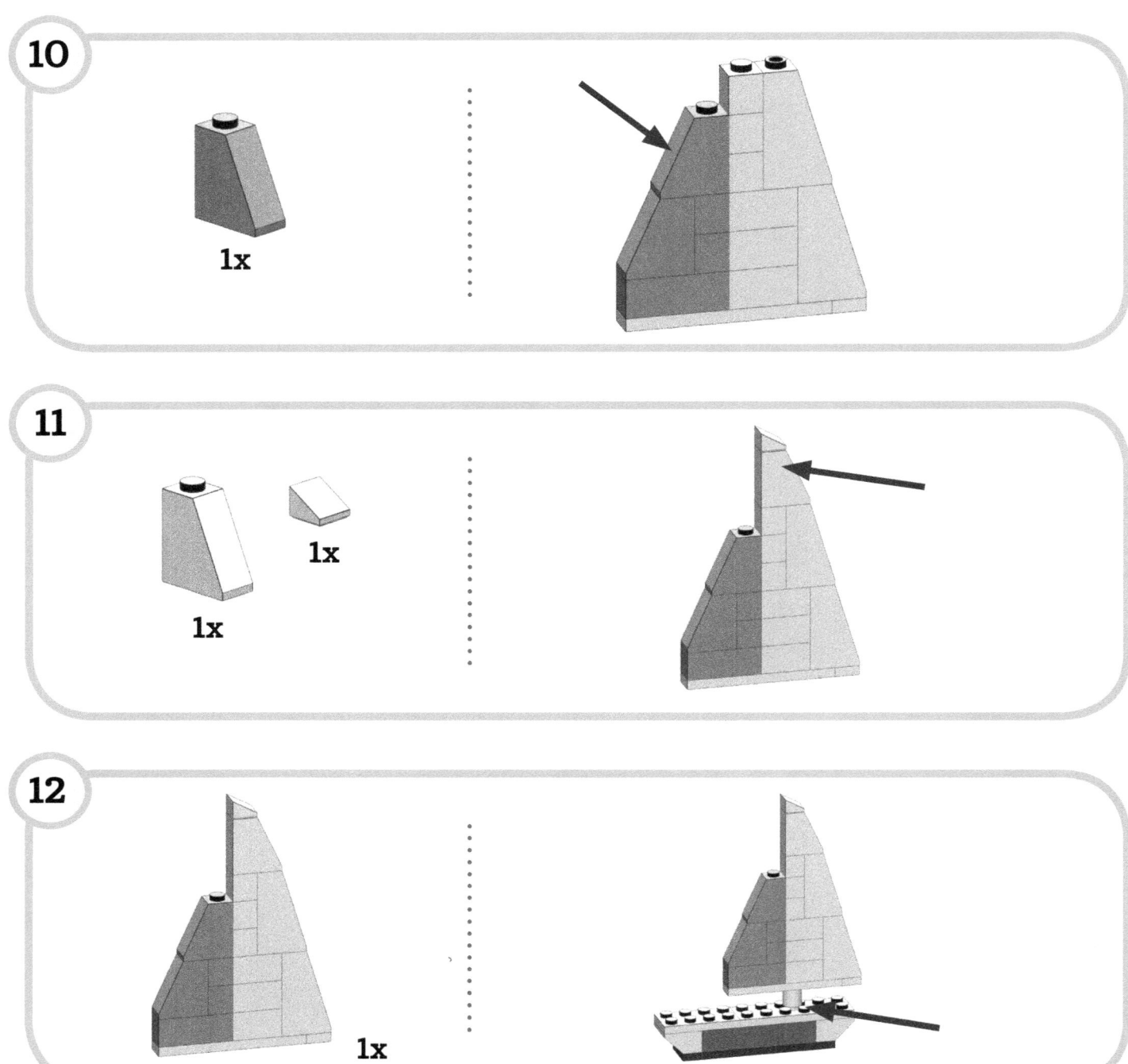

1x

11

1x

1x

12

1x

Build a Blue Sailboat

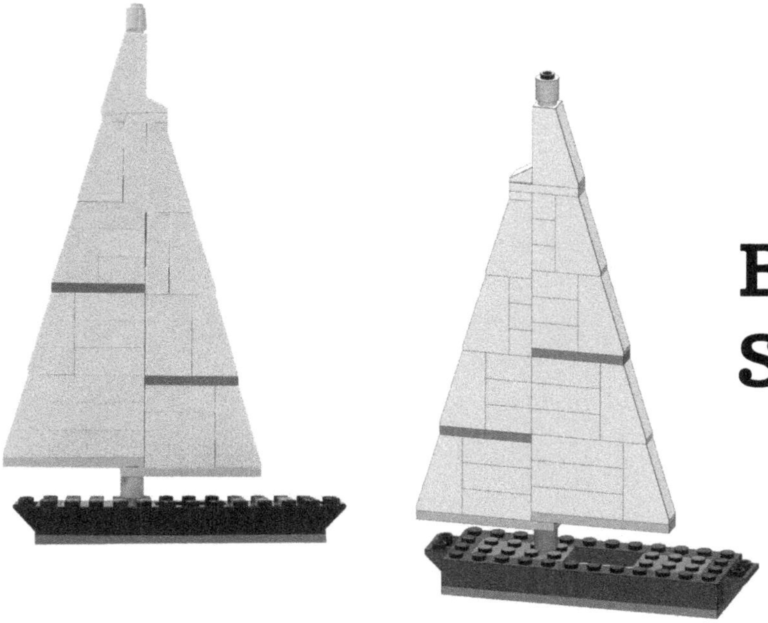

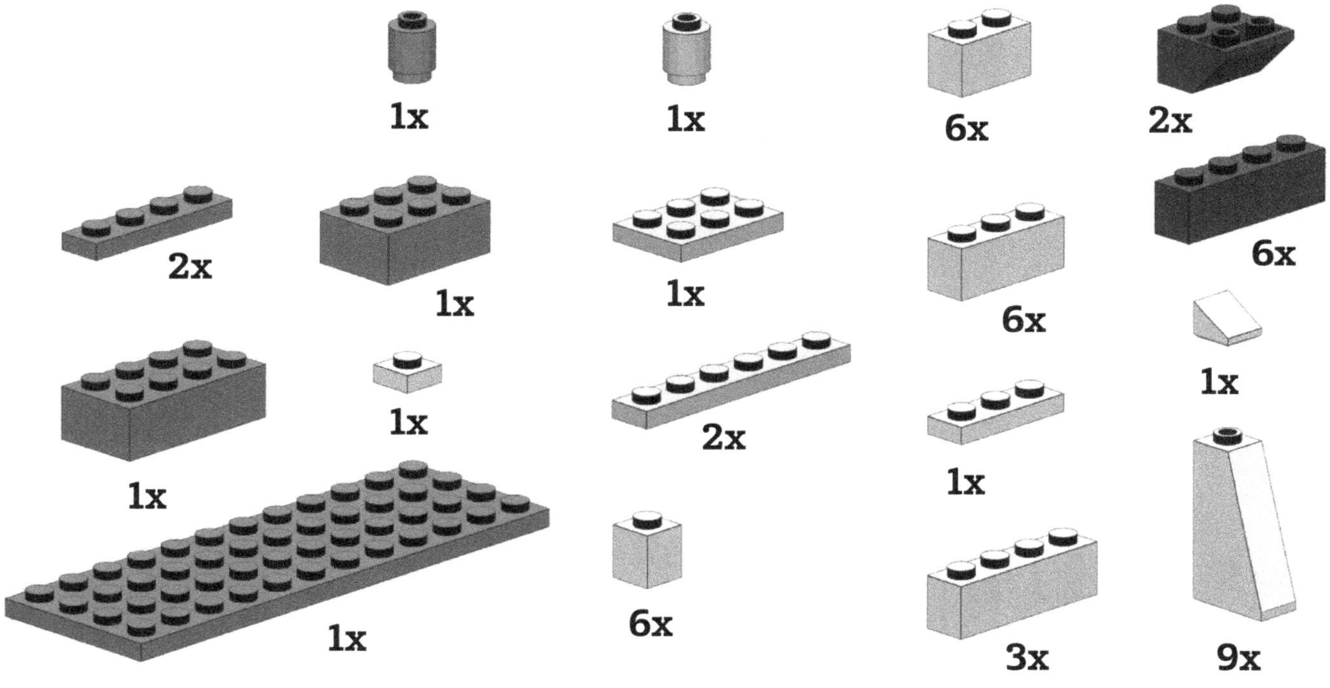

1x

1x

6x

2x

2x

1x

1x

6x

6x

1x

1x

2x

1x

1x

6x

3x

9x

1

1x

1x

3x

1x

1x

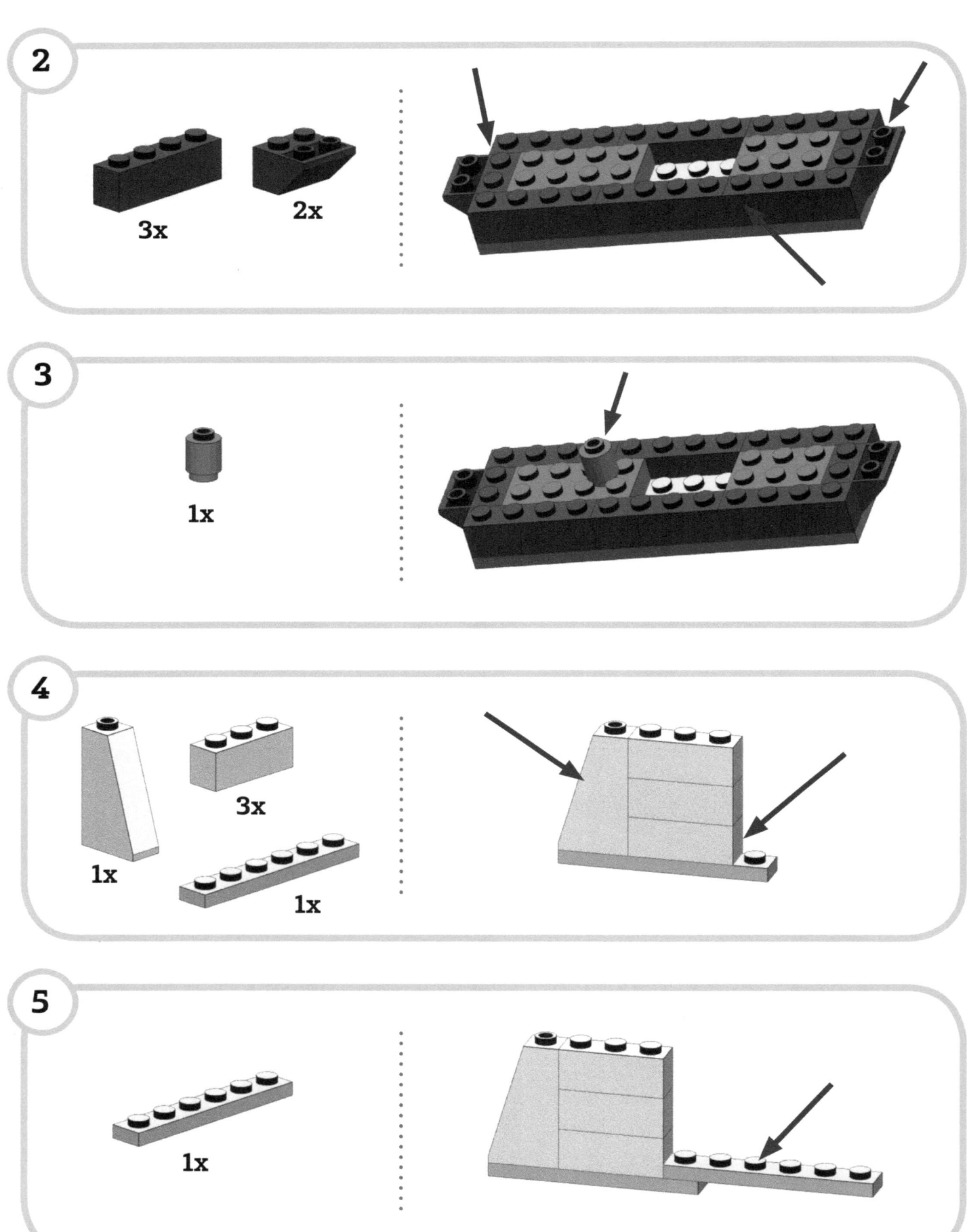

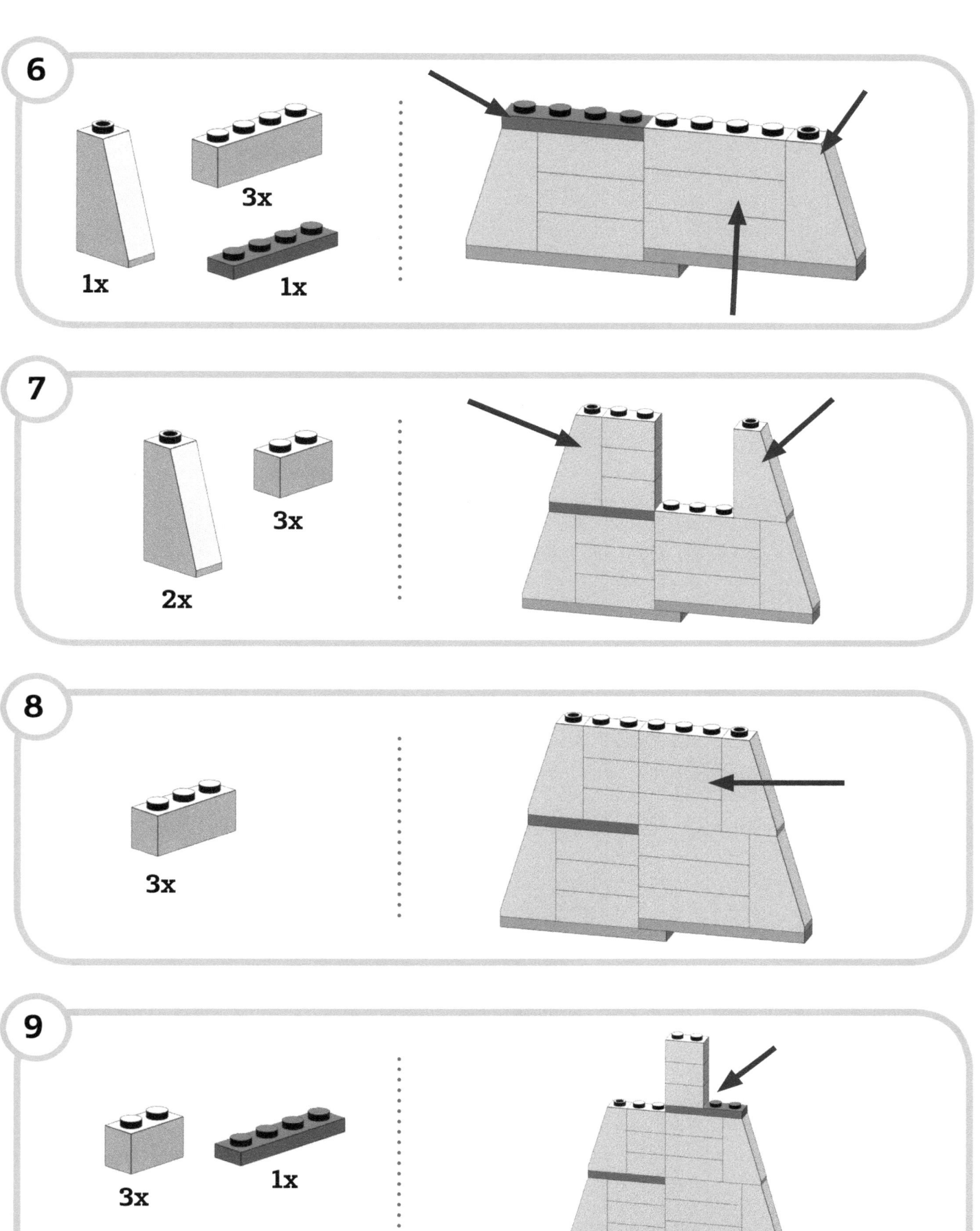

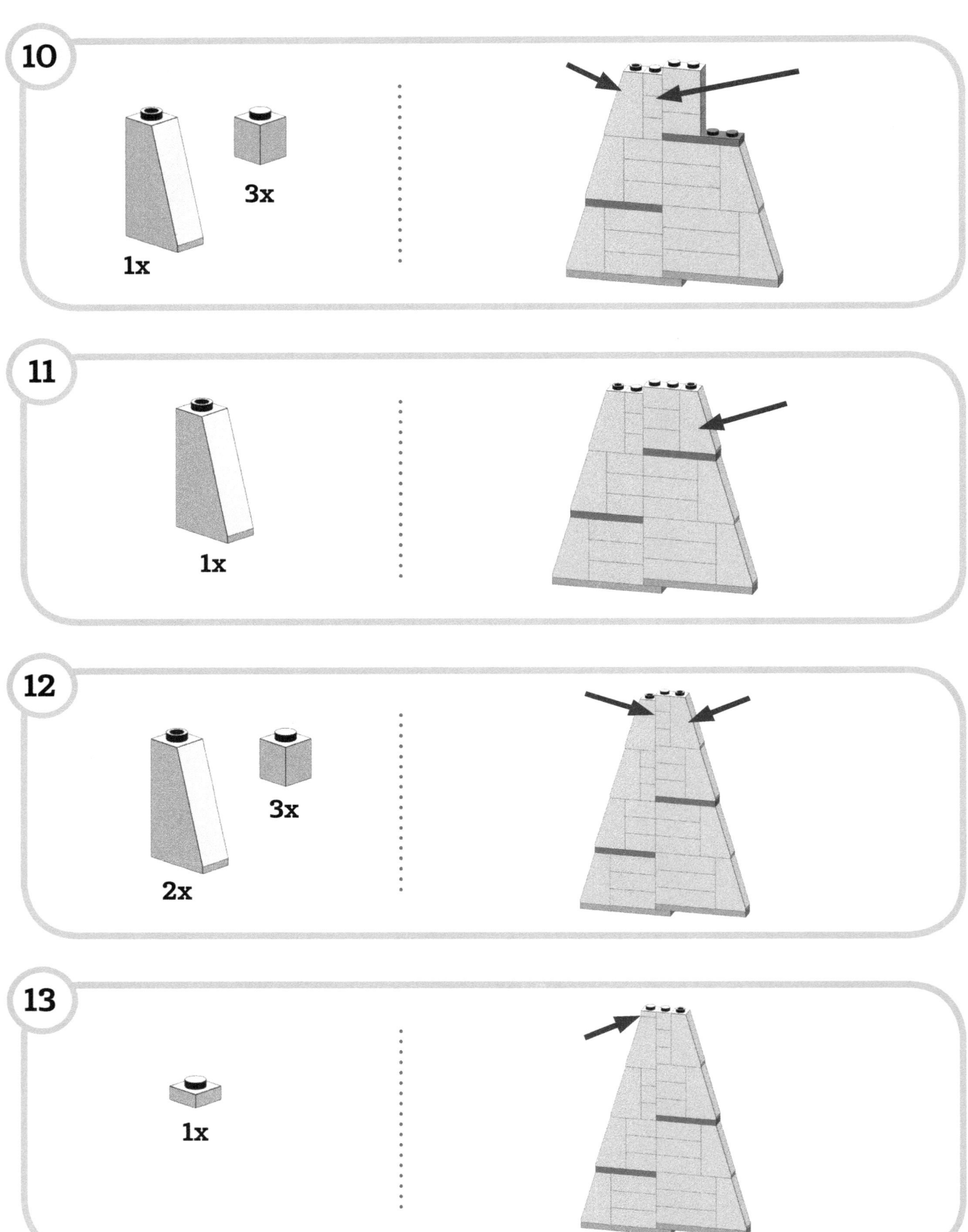

14

1x

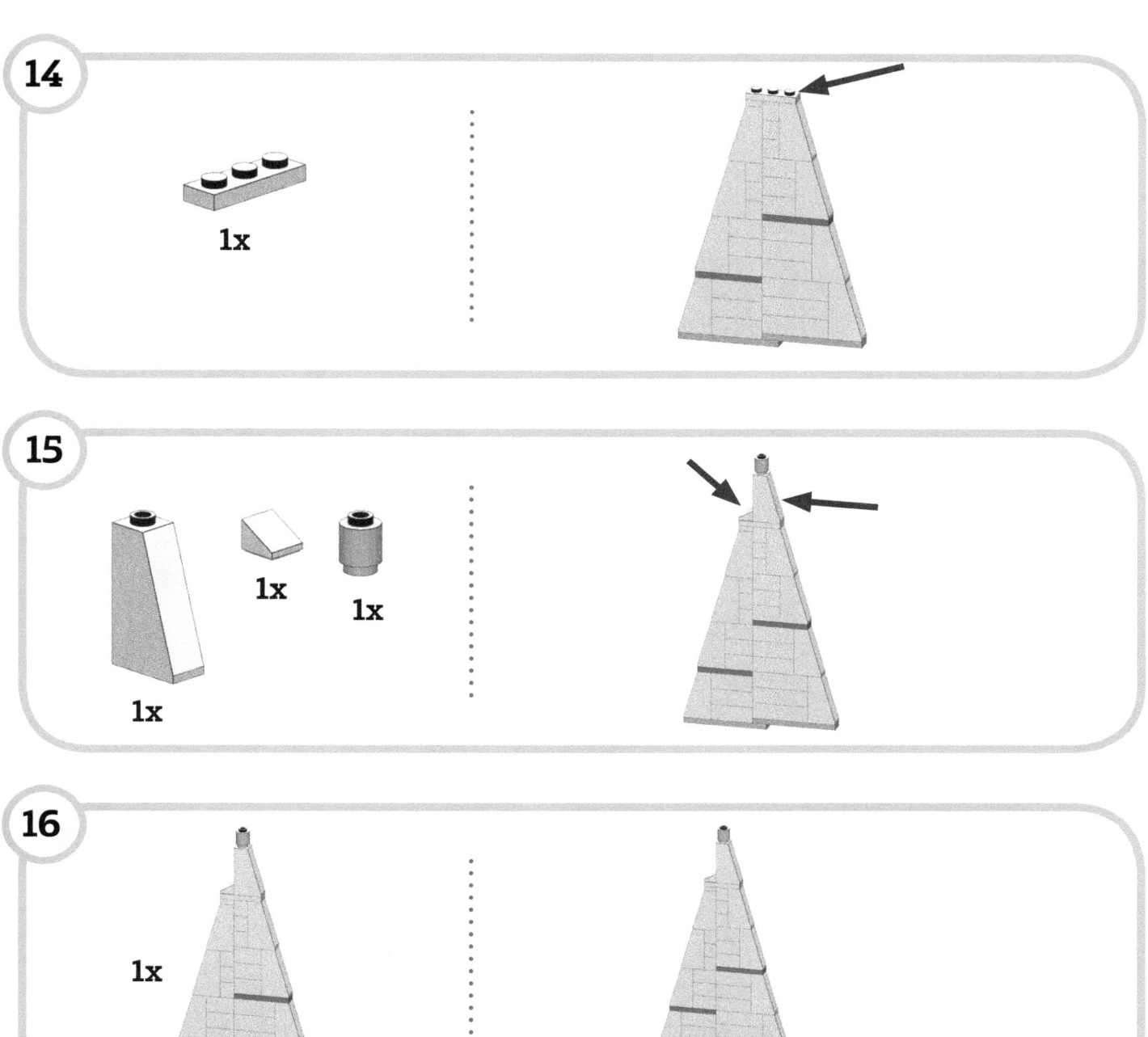

15

1x

1x

1x

16

1x

Sports Boats

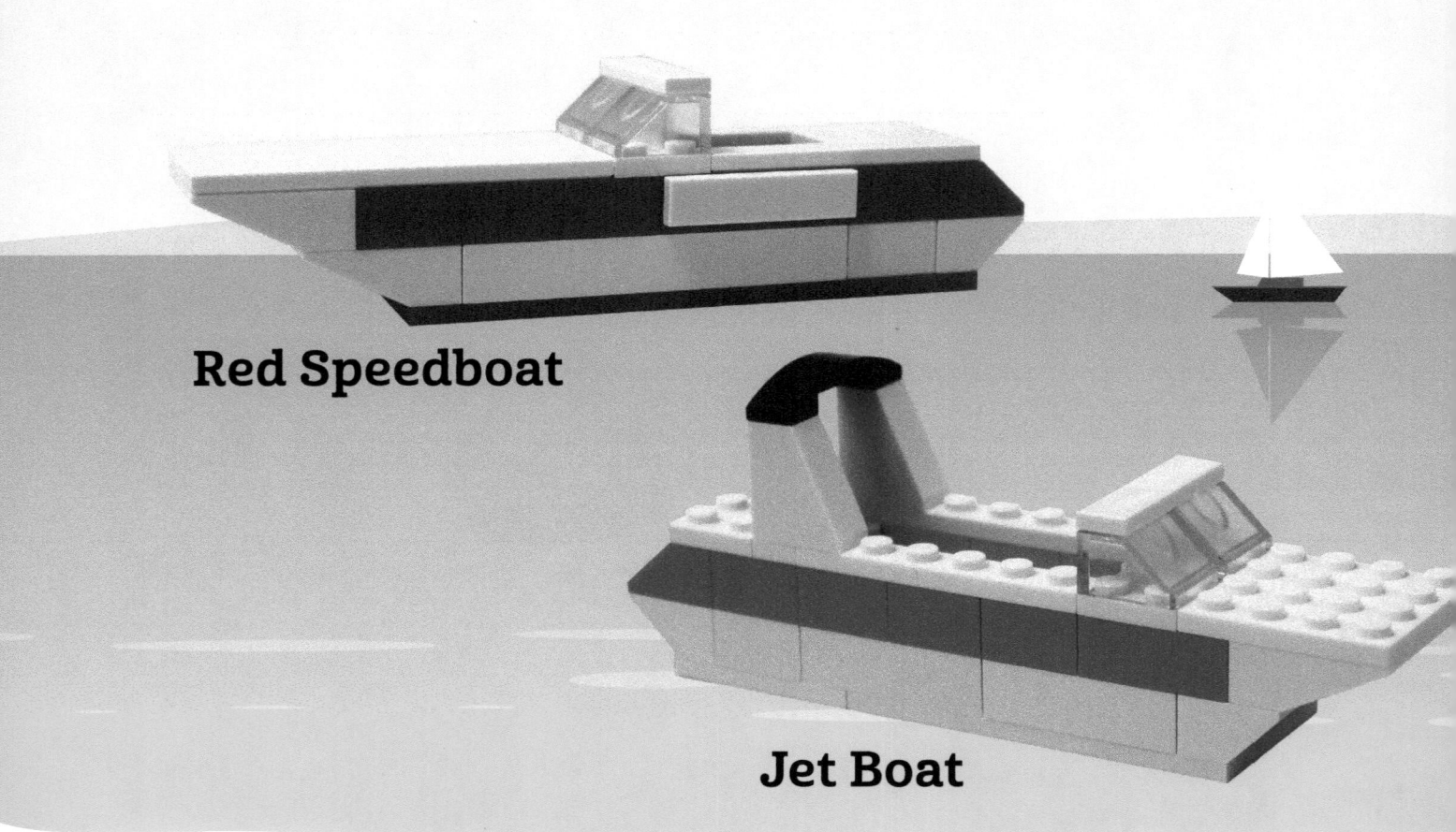

Red Speedboat

Jet Boat

**Orange Jet
Ski®**

Blue Jet Ski®

Build a Red Speedboat

1x
4x
2x
1x
2x
2x
1x
4x
2x
4x
4x
1x
1x
1x
3x
1x
2x

1
1x
2x

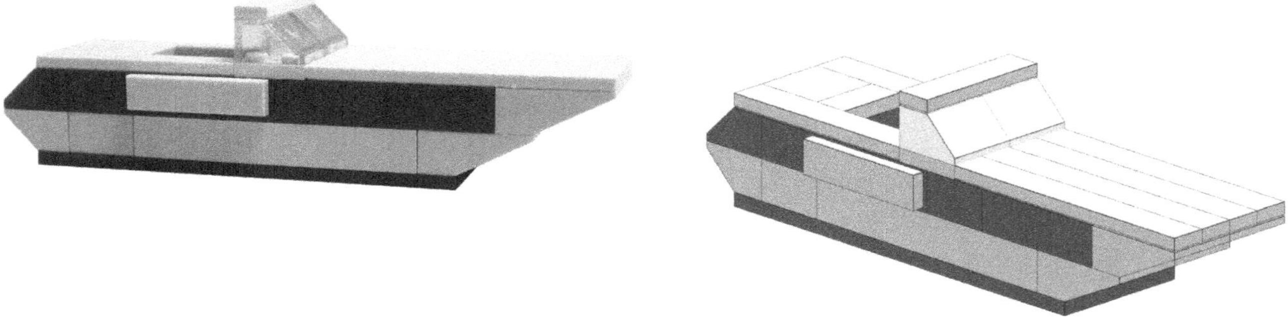

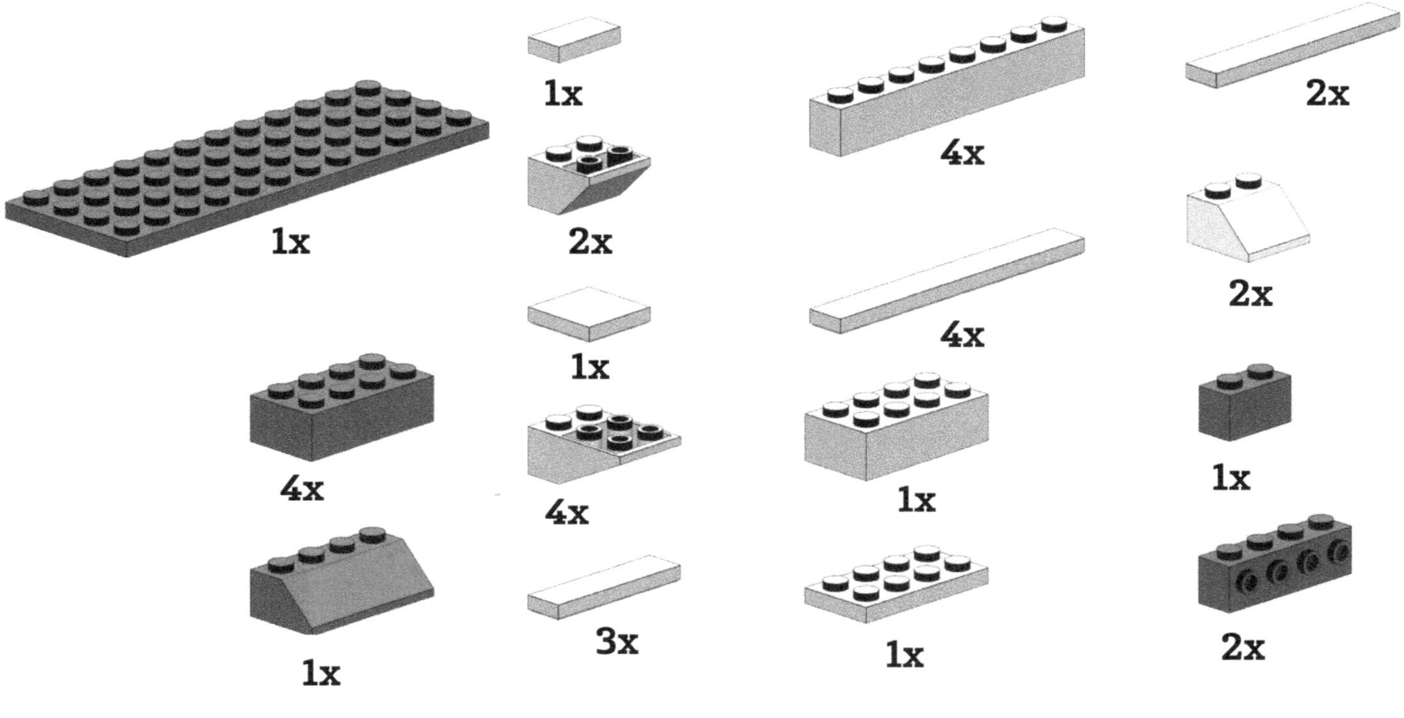

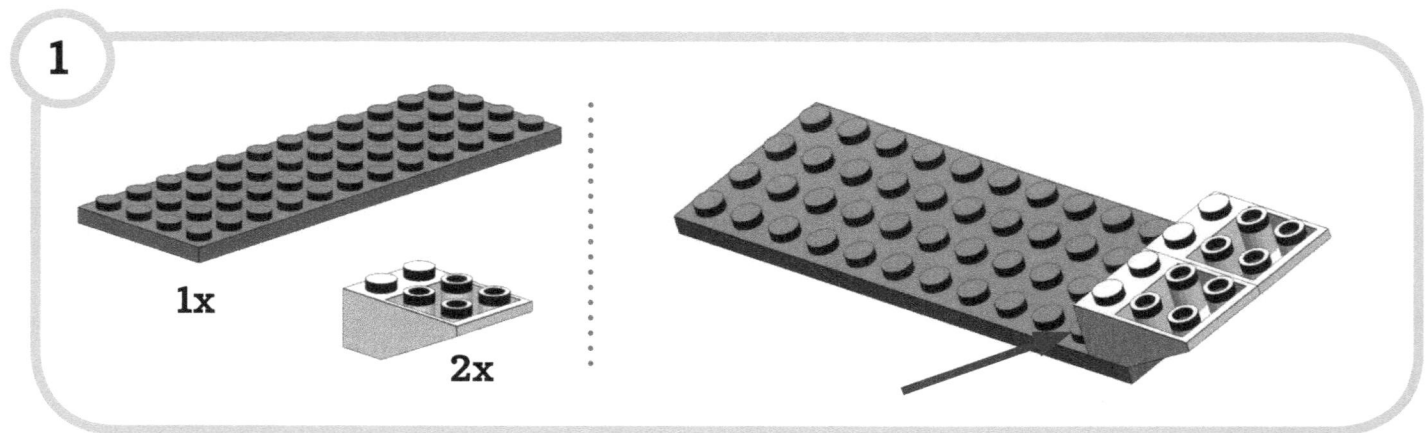

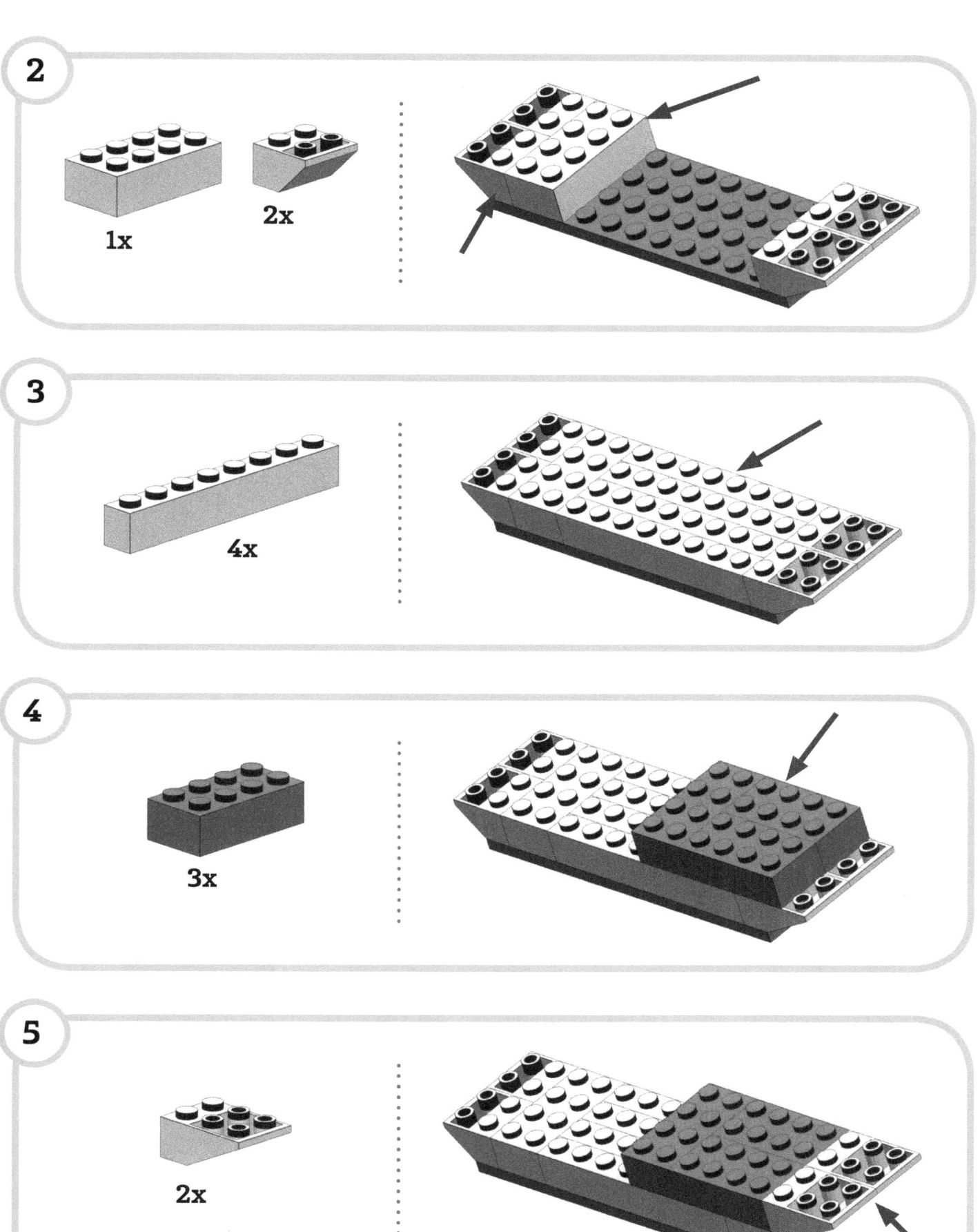

31

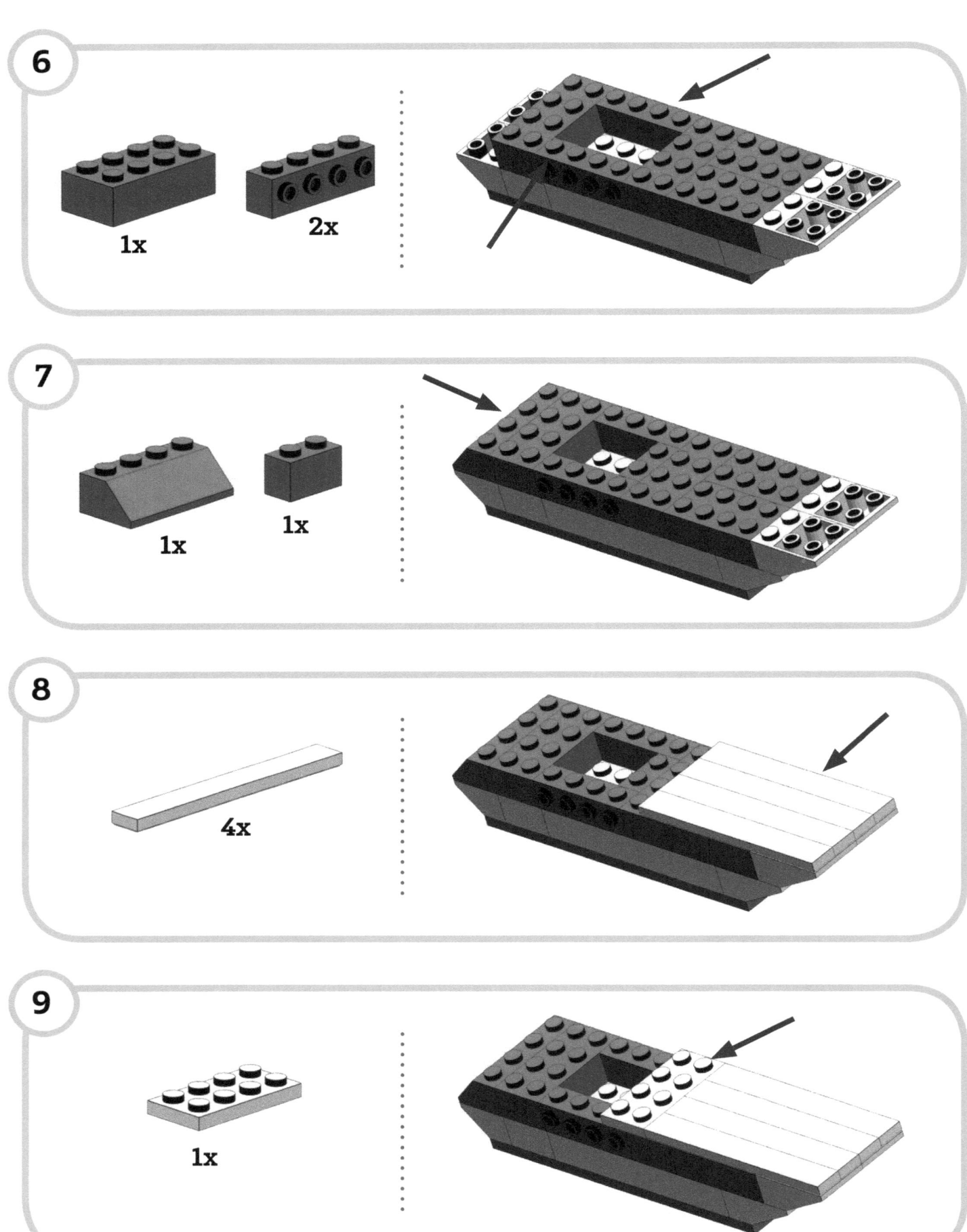

6 1x 2x

7 1x 1x

8 4x

9 1x

10

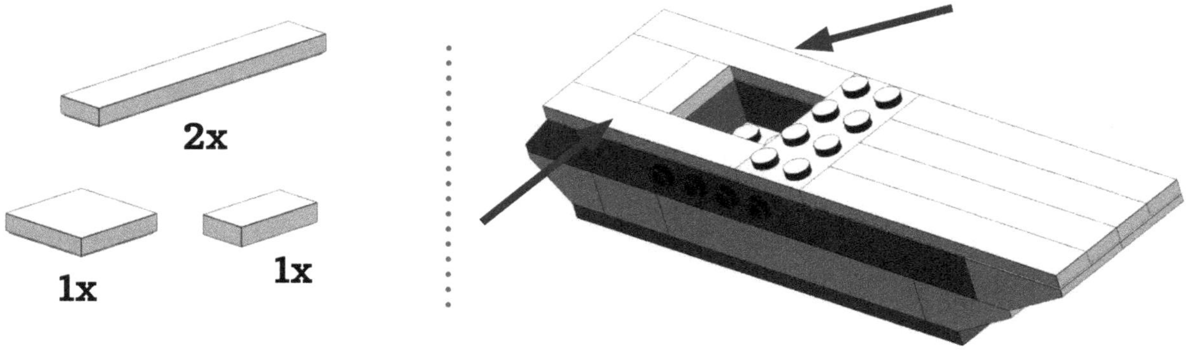

2x

1x 1x

11

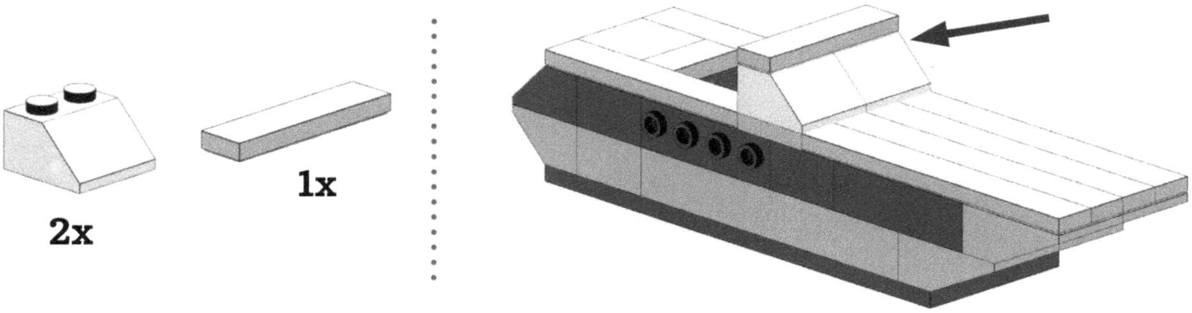

2x 1x

12

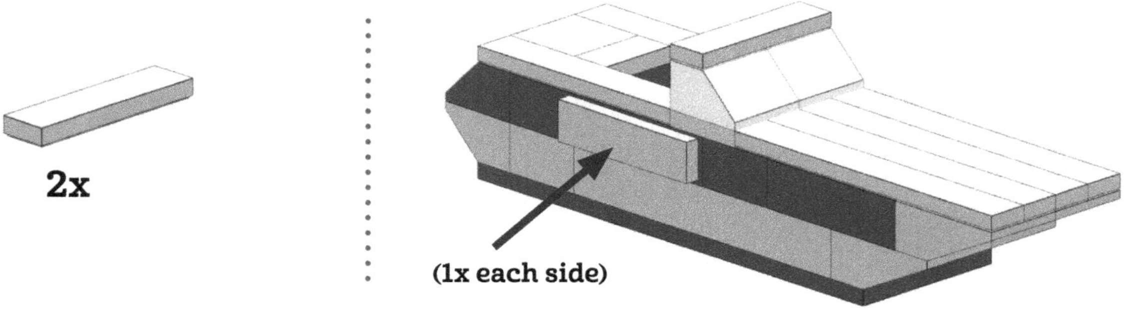

2x

(1x each side)

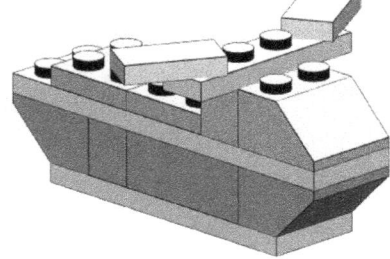

Build an Orange Jet Ski®

2x

2x

1x

1x

1x

1x

2x

1x

1

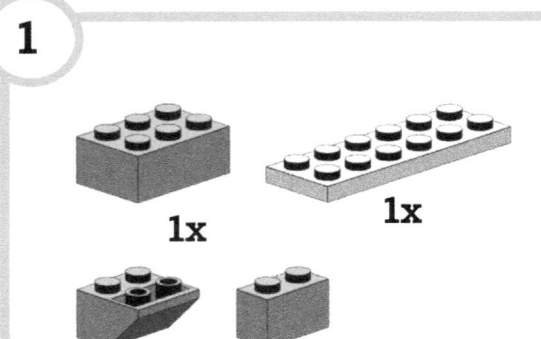

1x

1x

2x

1x

2

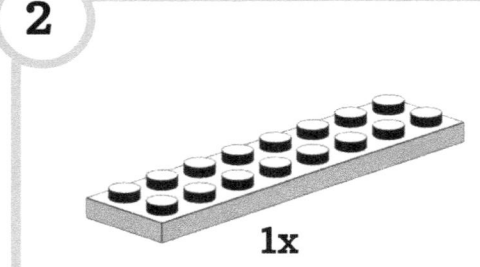

1x

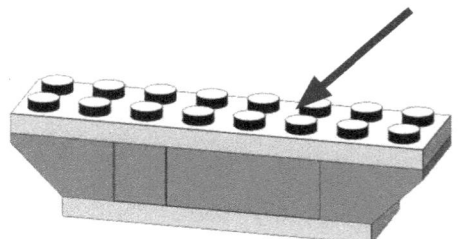

3

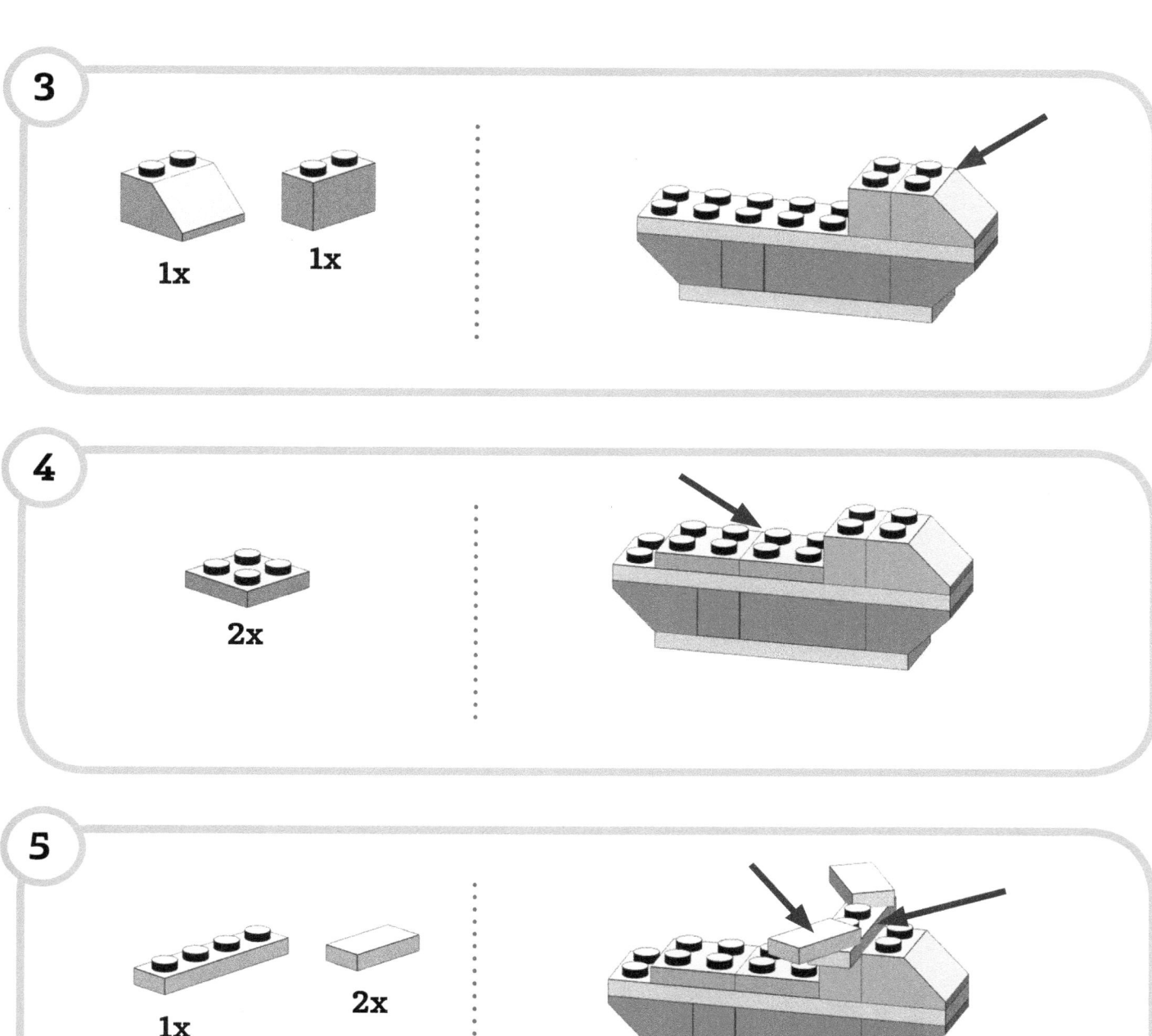

1x 1x

4

2x

5

1x 2x

Build a Blue Jet Ski®

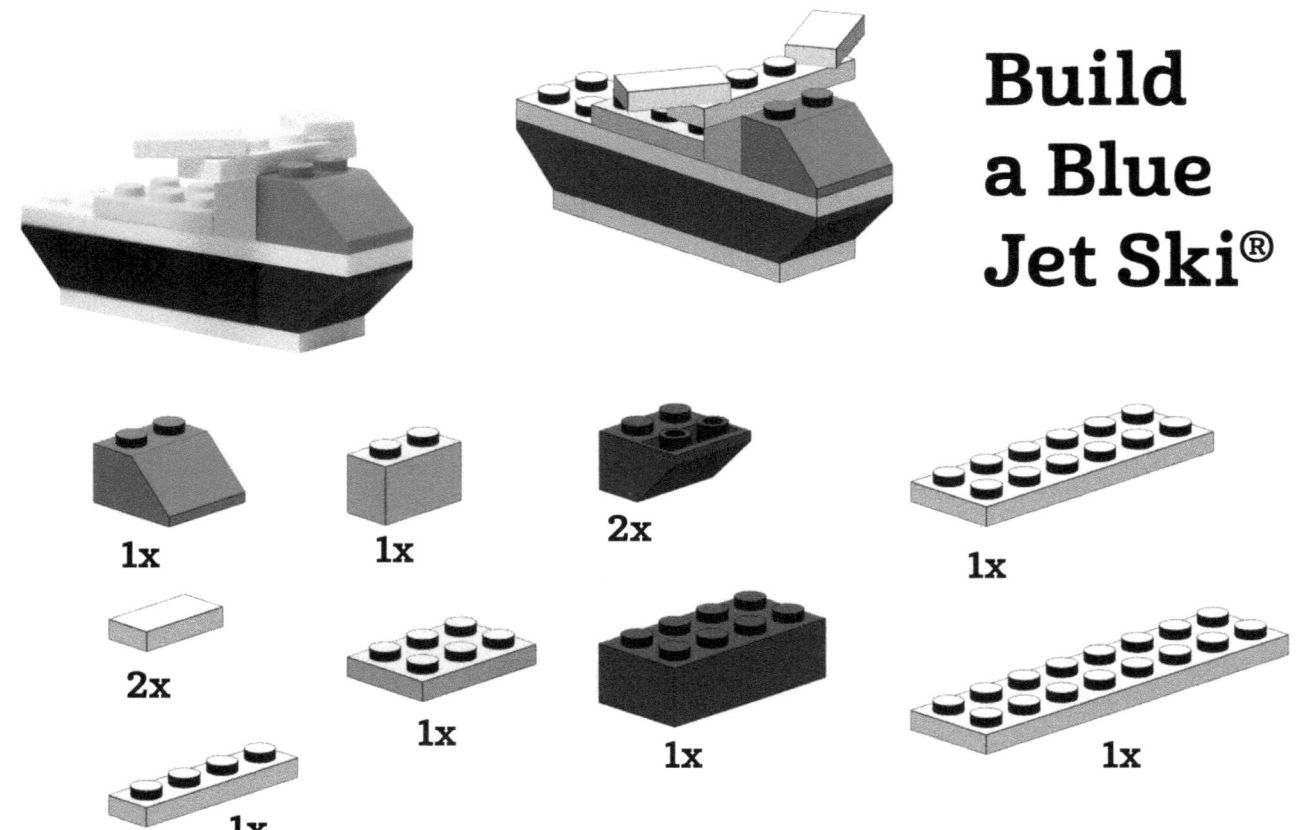

1x 1x 2x 1x 2x 1x 1x 1x 1x

1

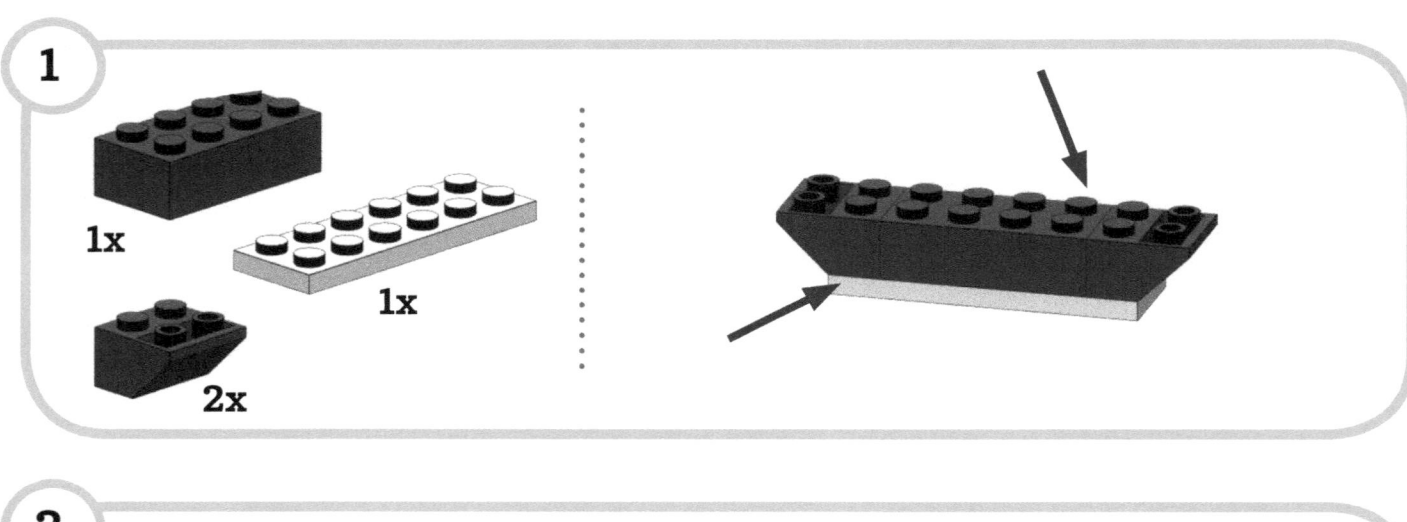

1x 1x 2x

2

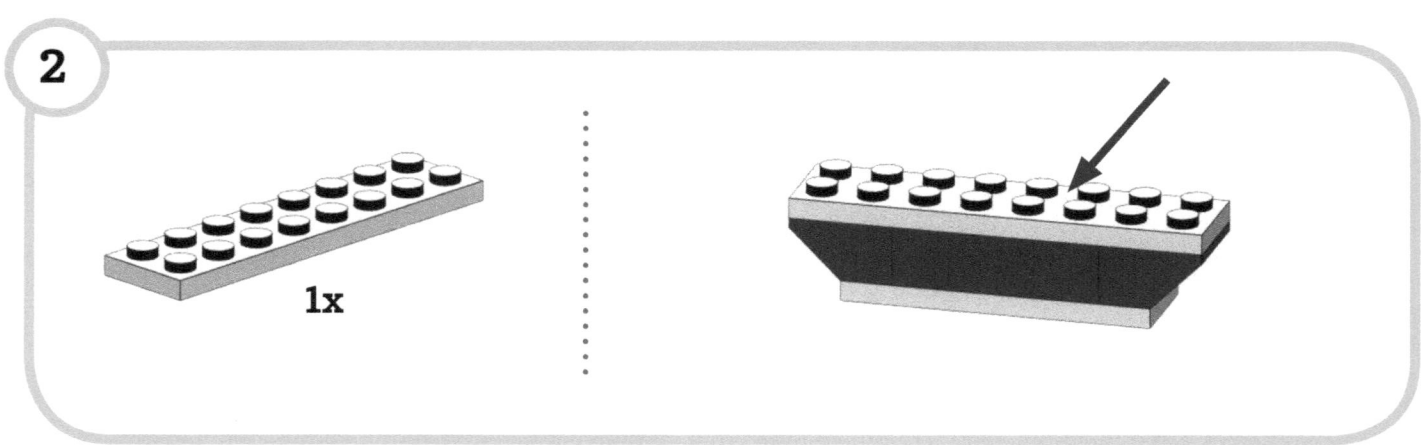

1x

3

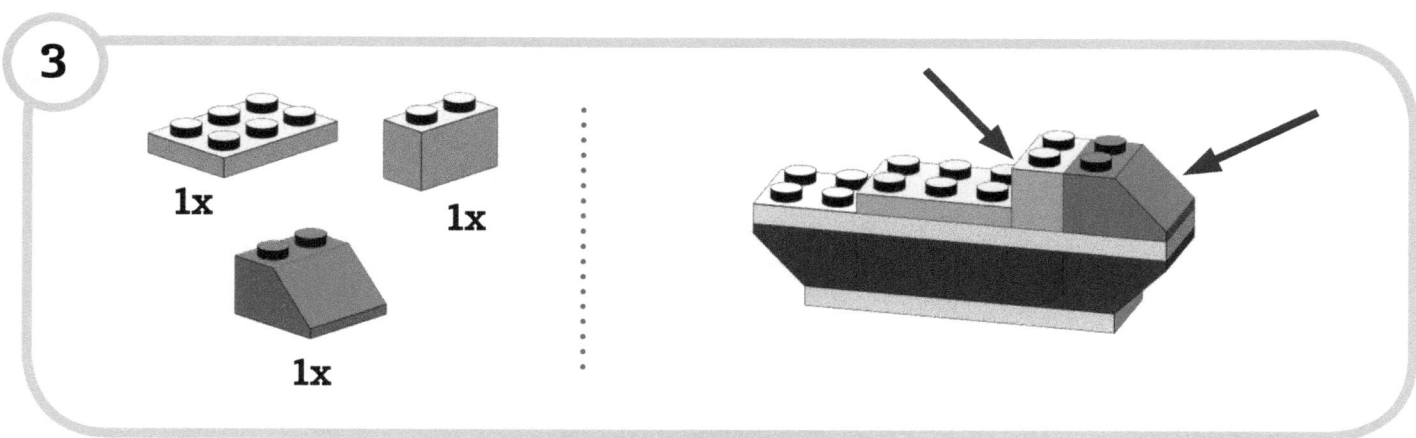

1x   1x

1x

4

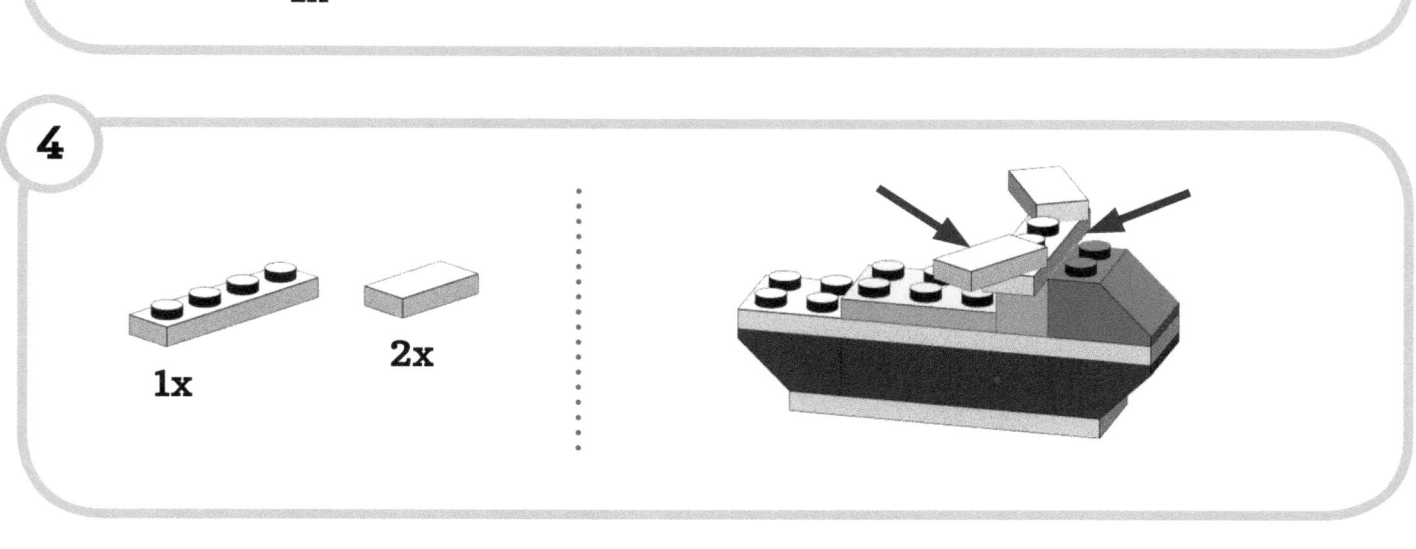

1x   2x

Build a
Jet Boat

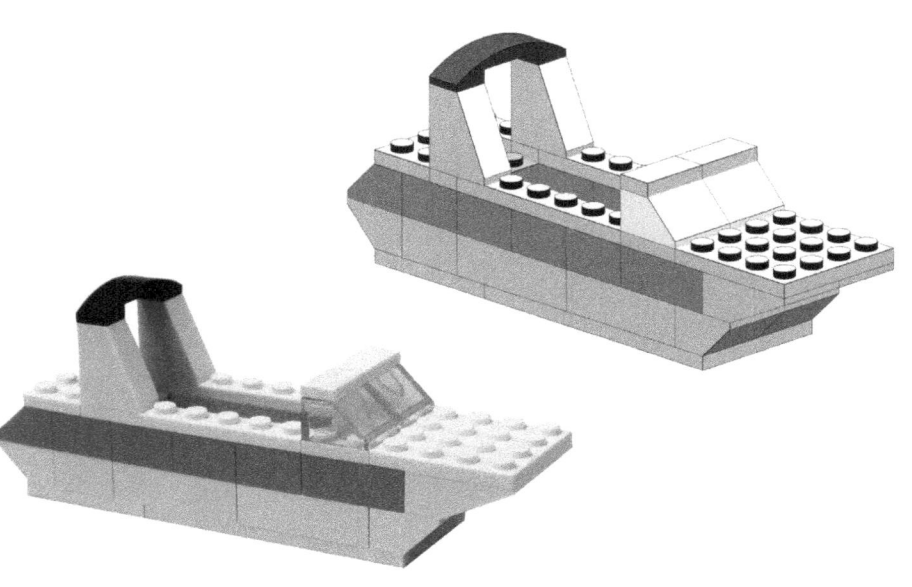

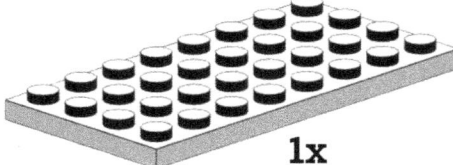

1x

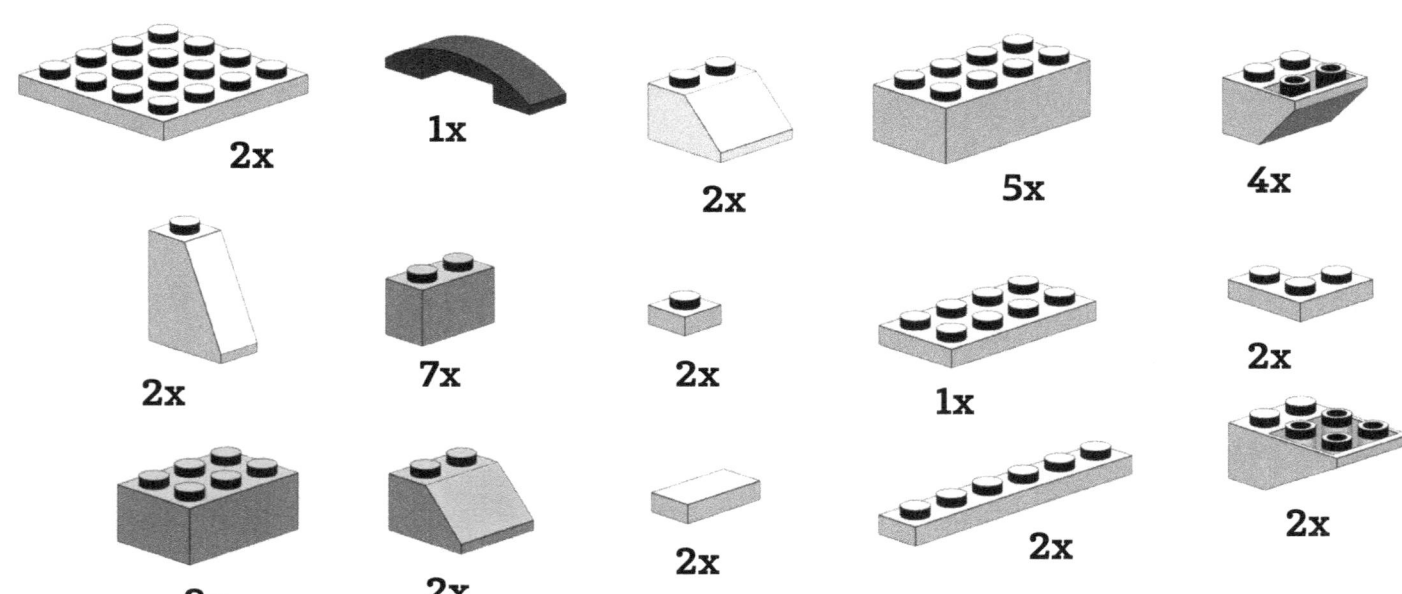

2x
1x
2x
5x
4x

2x
7x
2x
1x
2x

3x
2x
2x
2x
2x

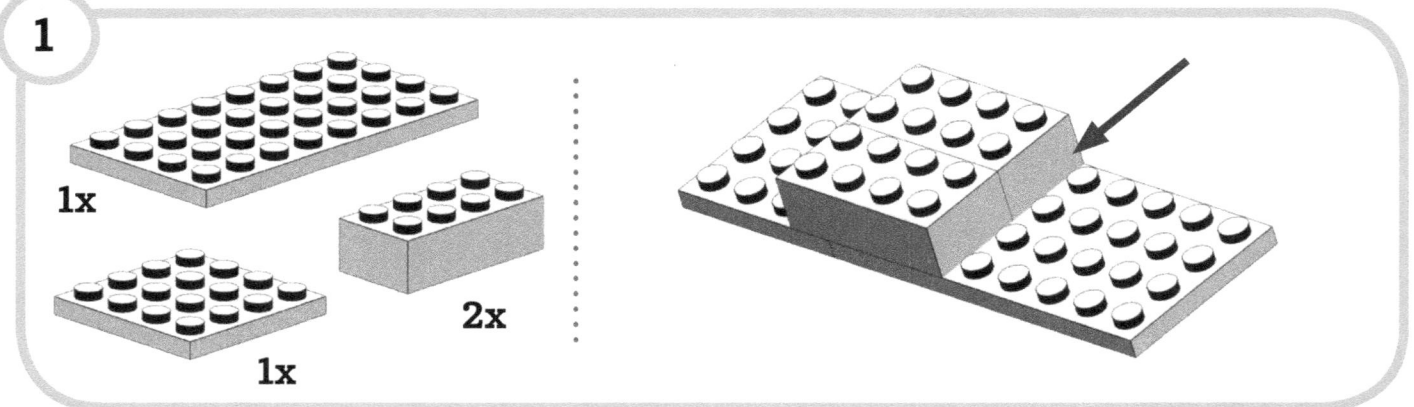

1

1x

2x

1x

38

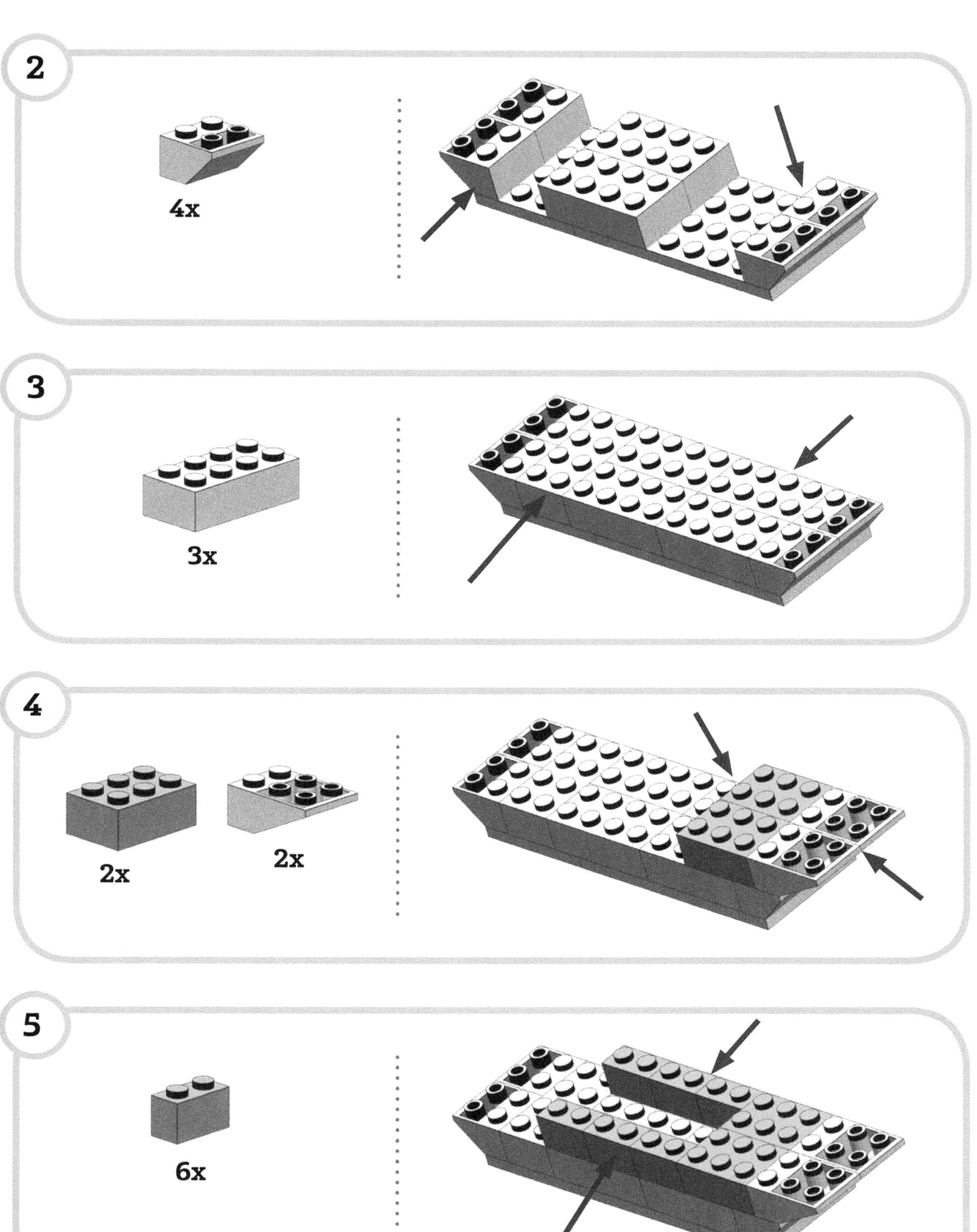

2 4x

3 3x

4 2x 2x

5 6x

39

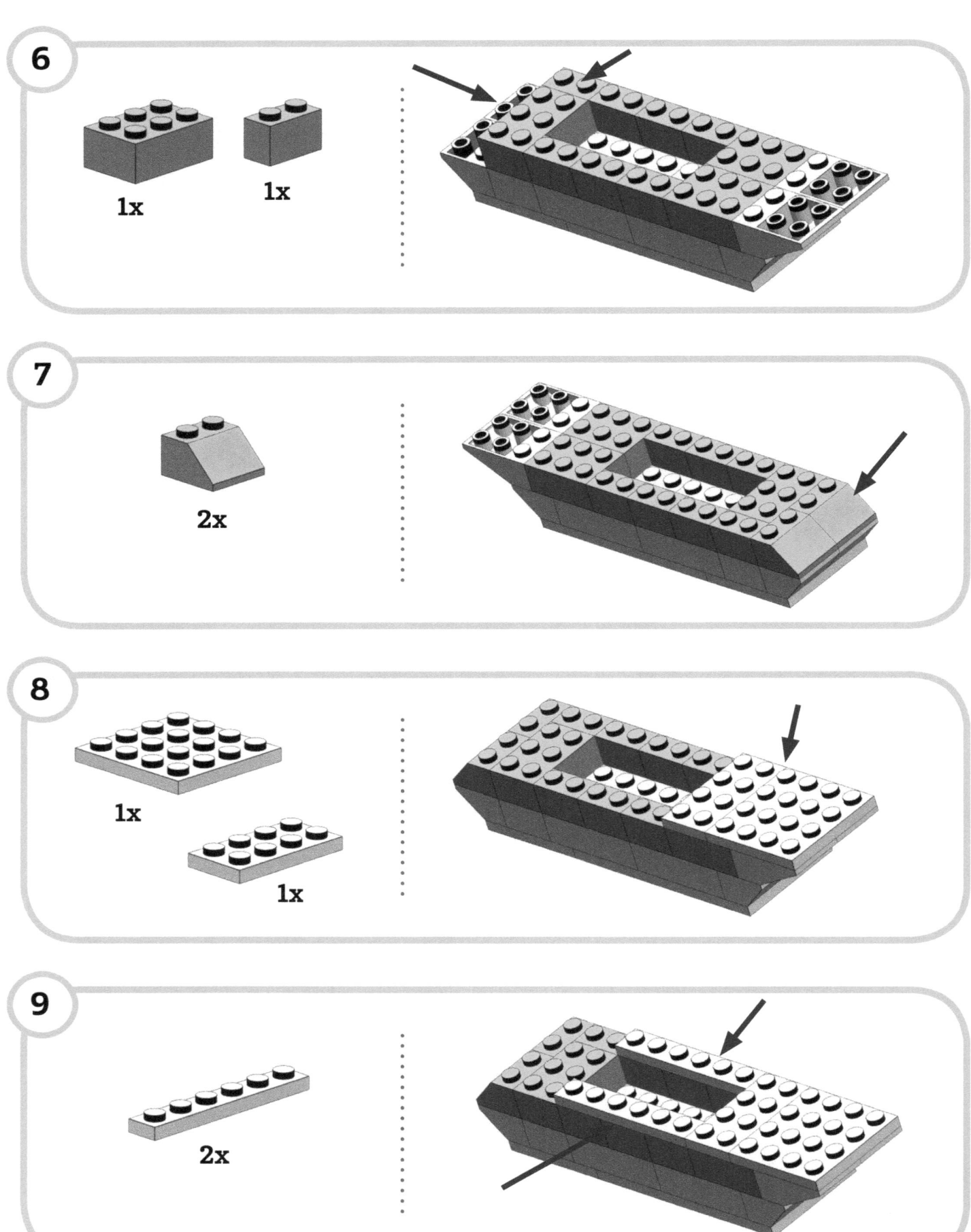

10

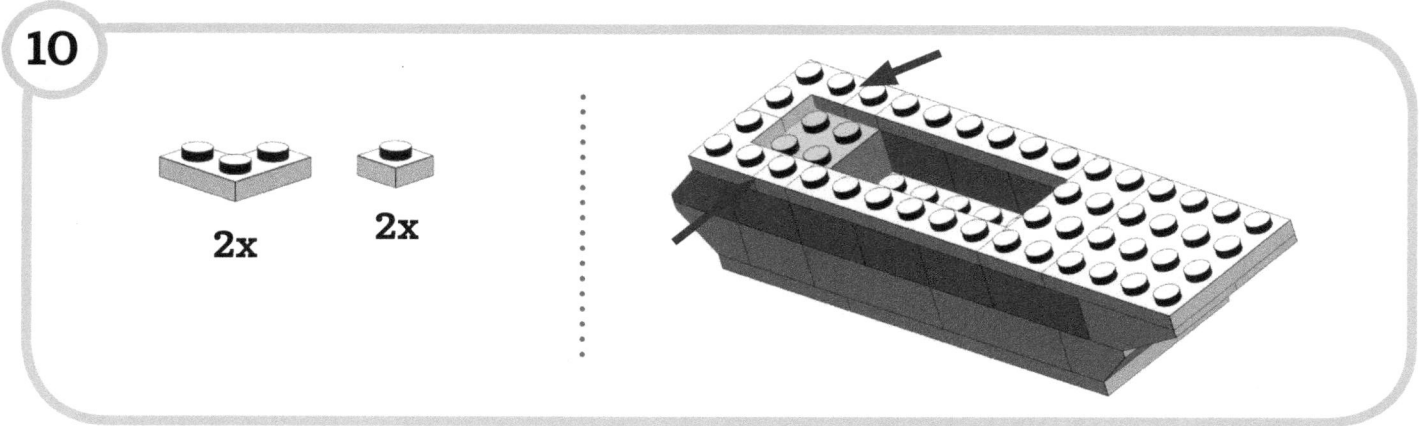

2x   2x

11

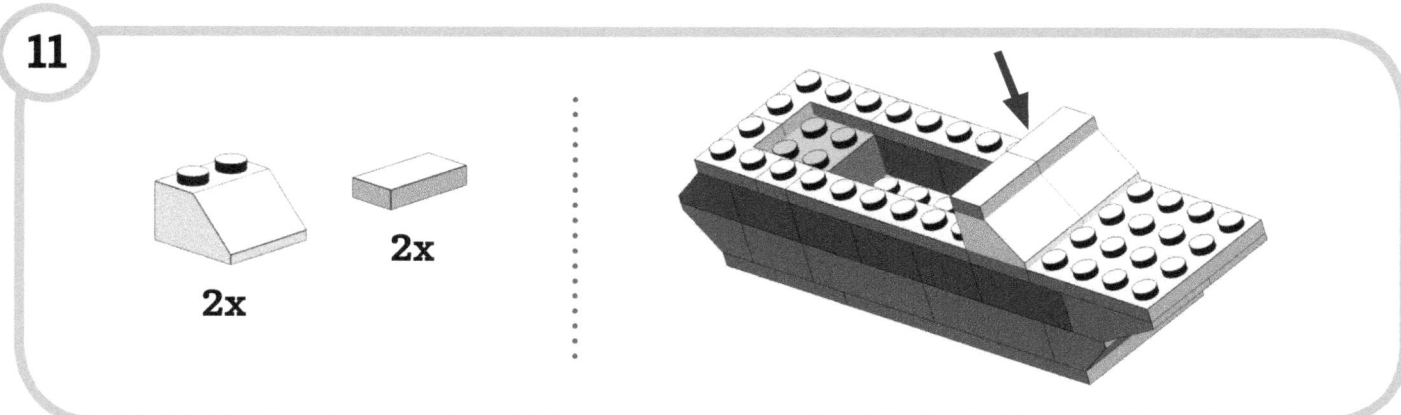

2x   2x

12

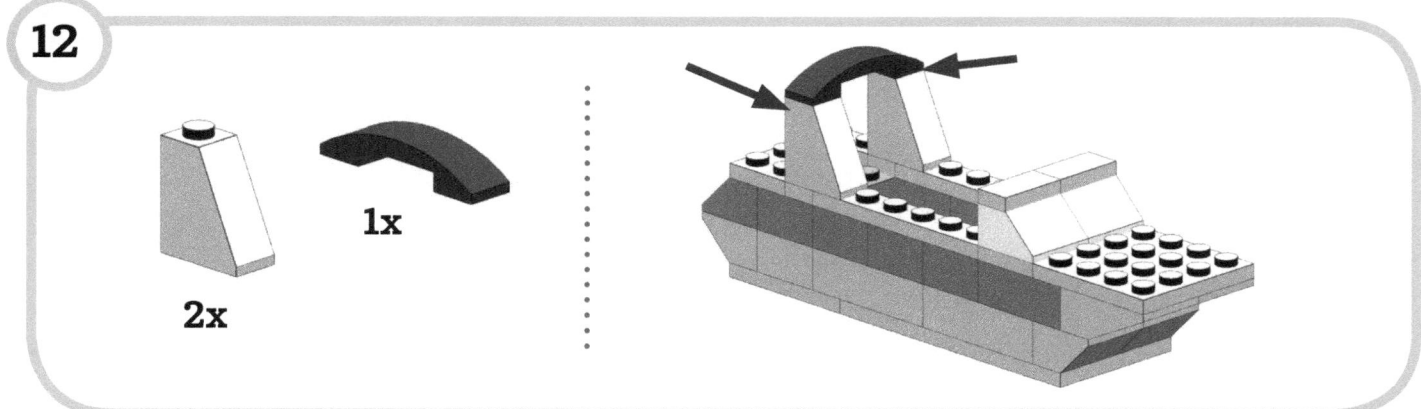

2x   1x

Boat-a-palooza

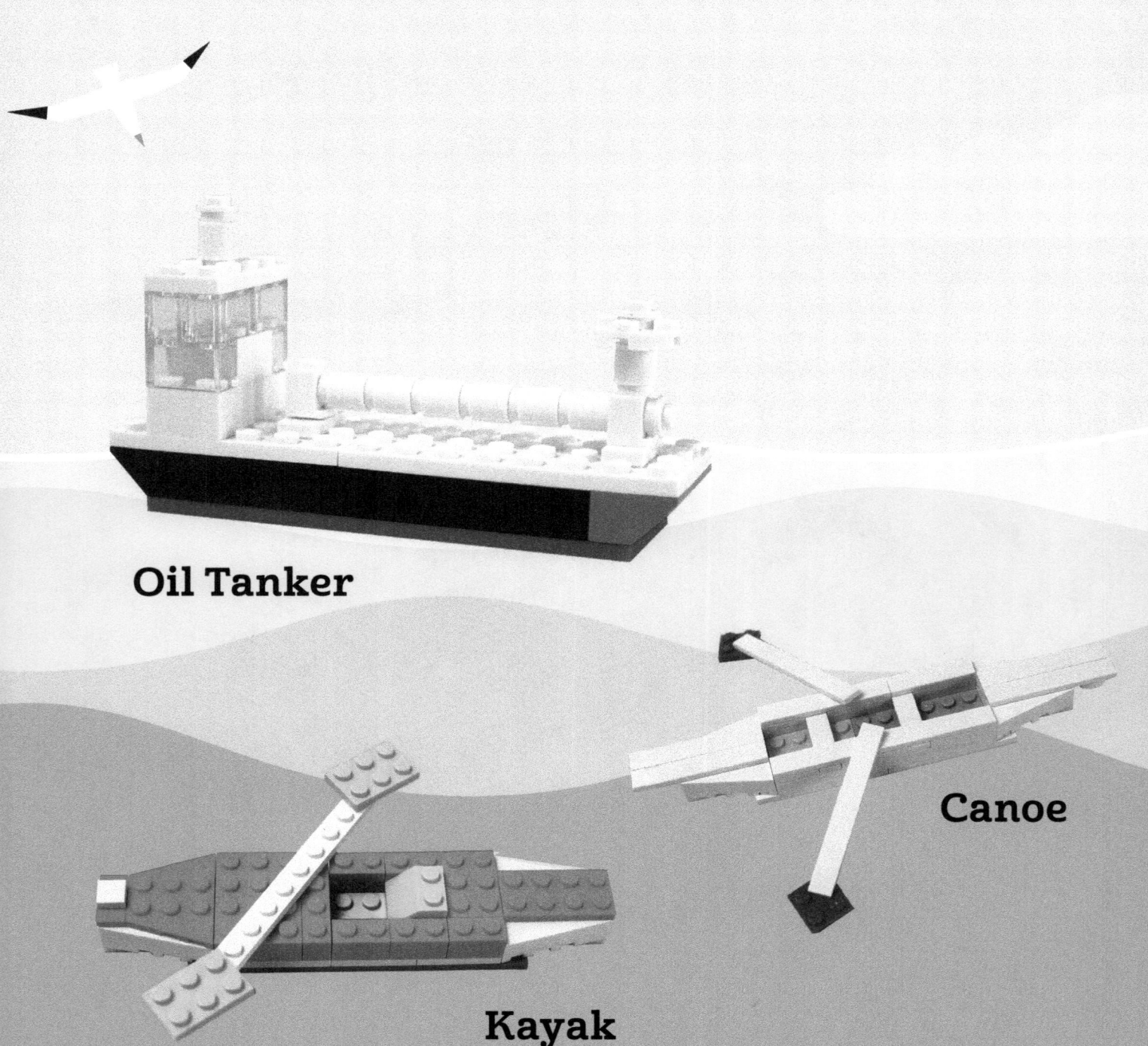

Oil Tanker

Canoe

Kayak

Super Yacht

Trimaran

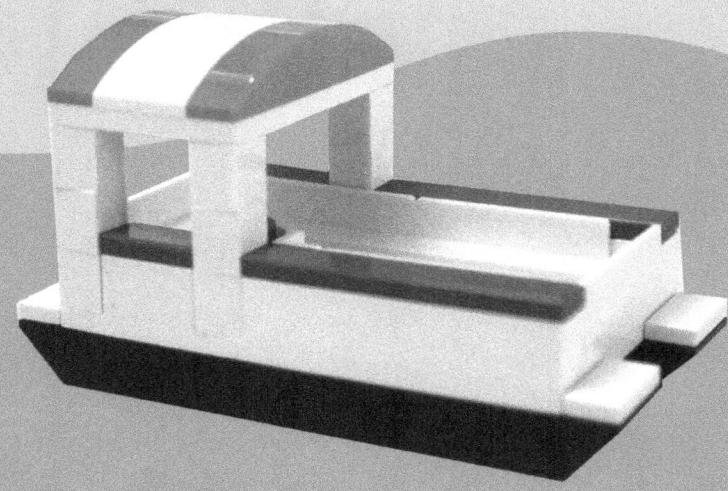

Pontoon

Build an Oil Tanker

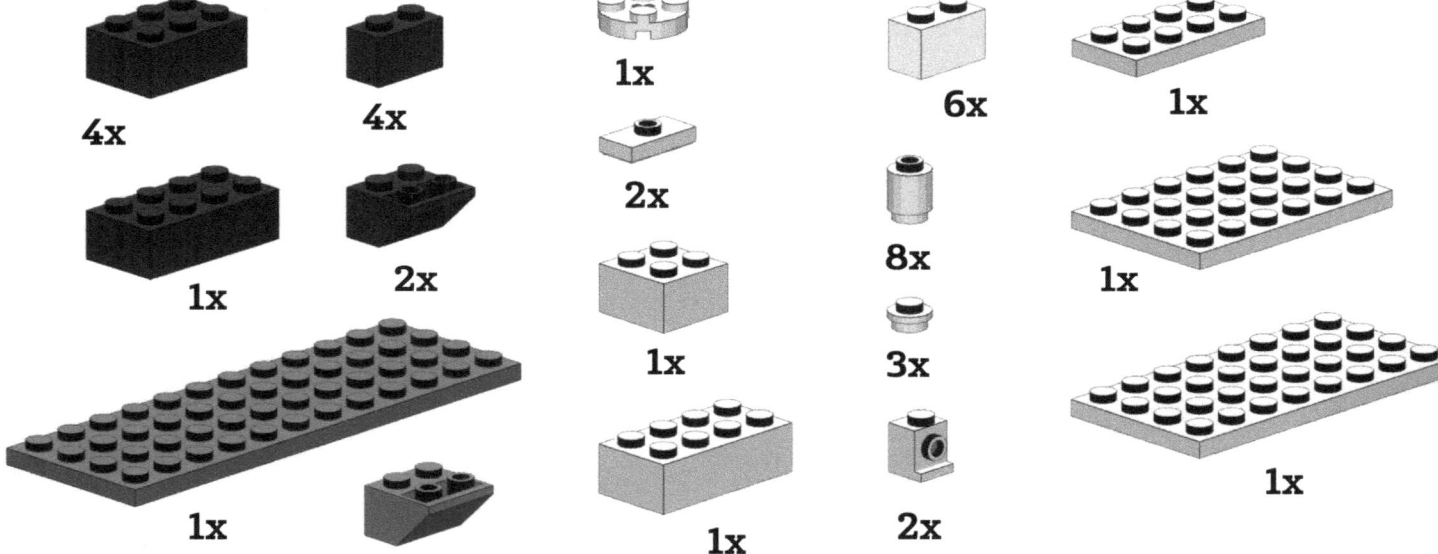

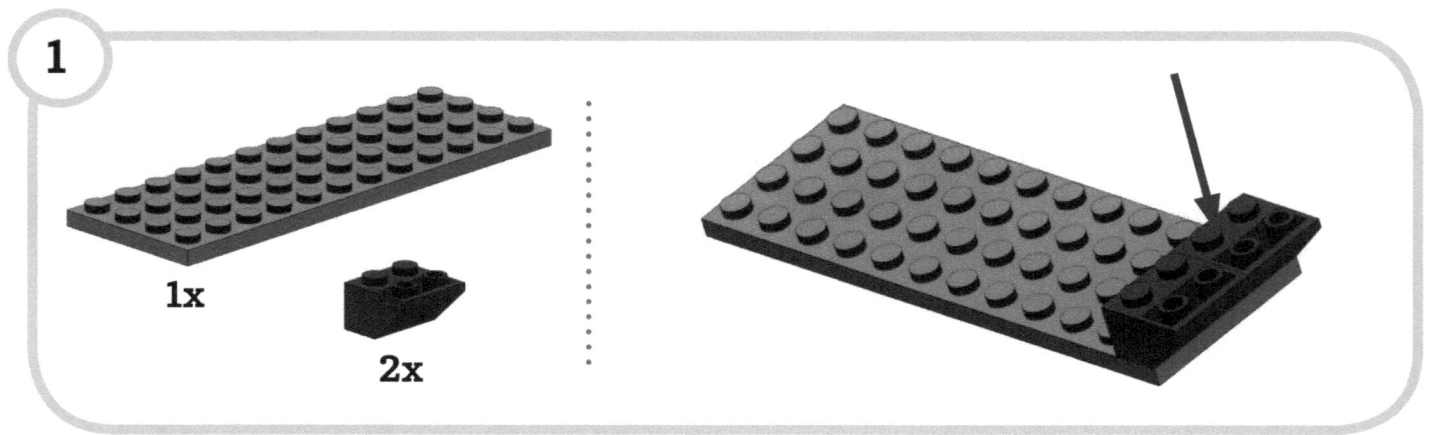

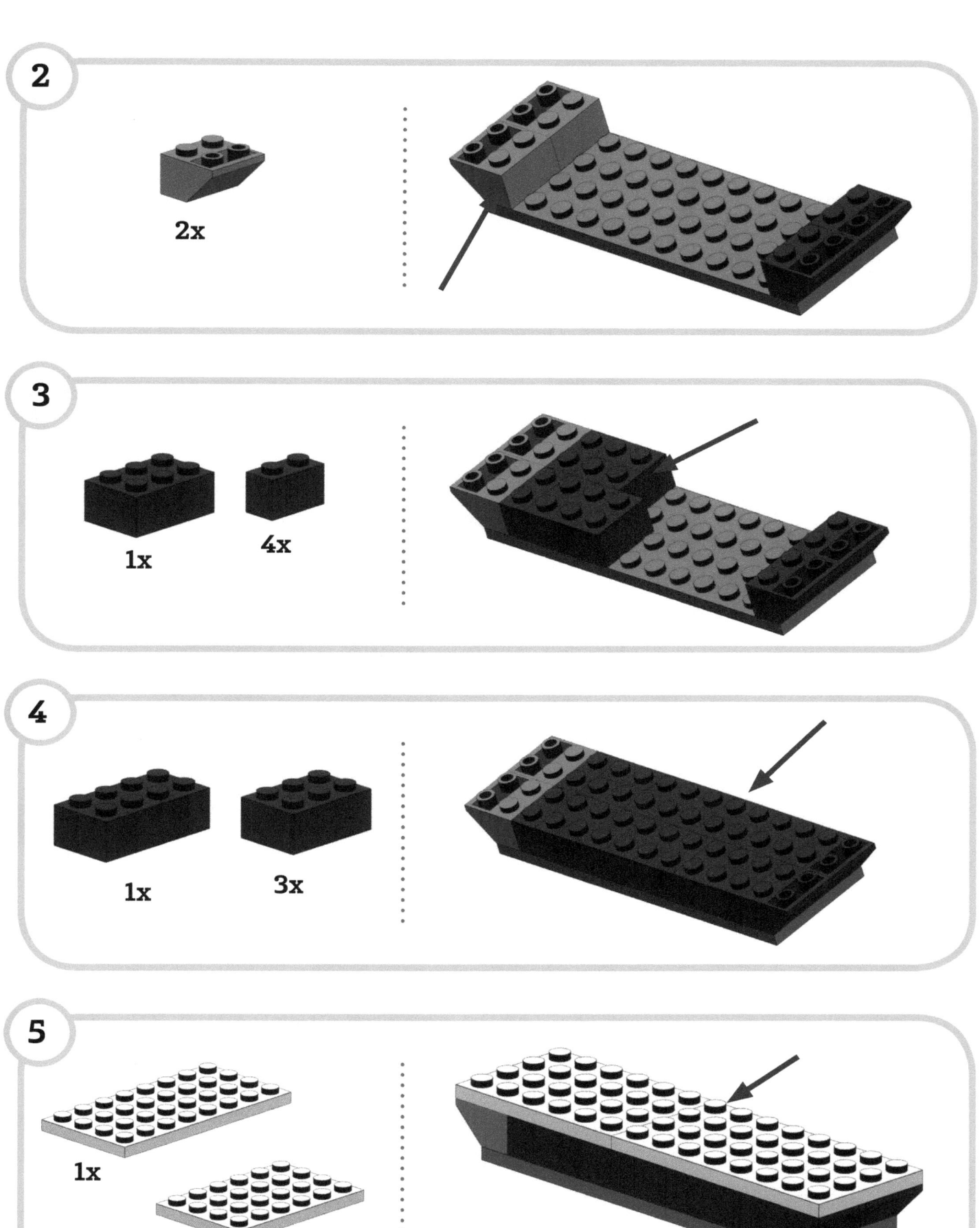

2

2x

3

1x 4x

4

1x 3x

5

1x

1x

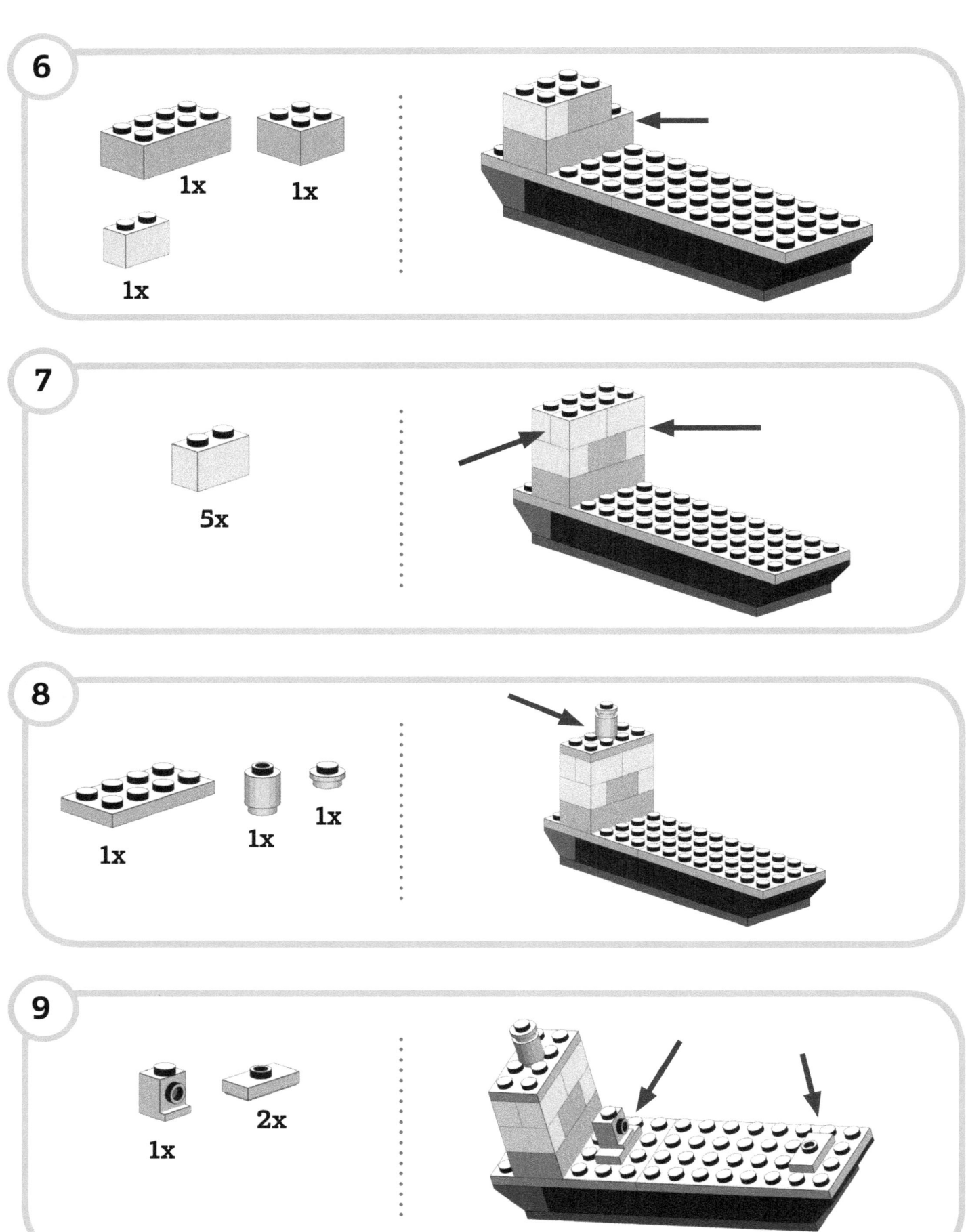

6 1x 1x 1x

7 5x

8 1x 1x 1x

9 1x 2x

10

6x

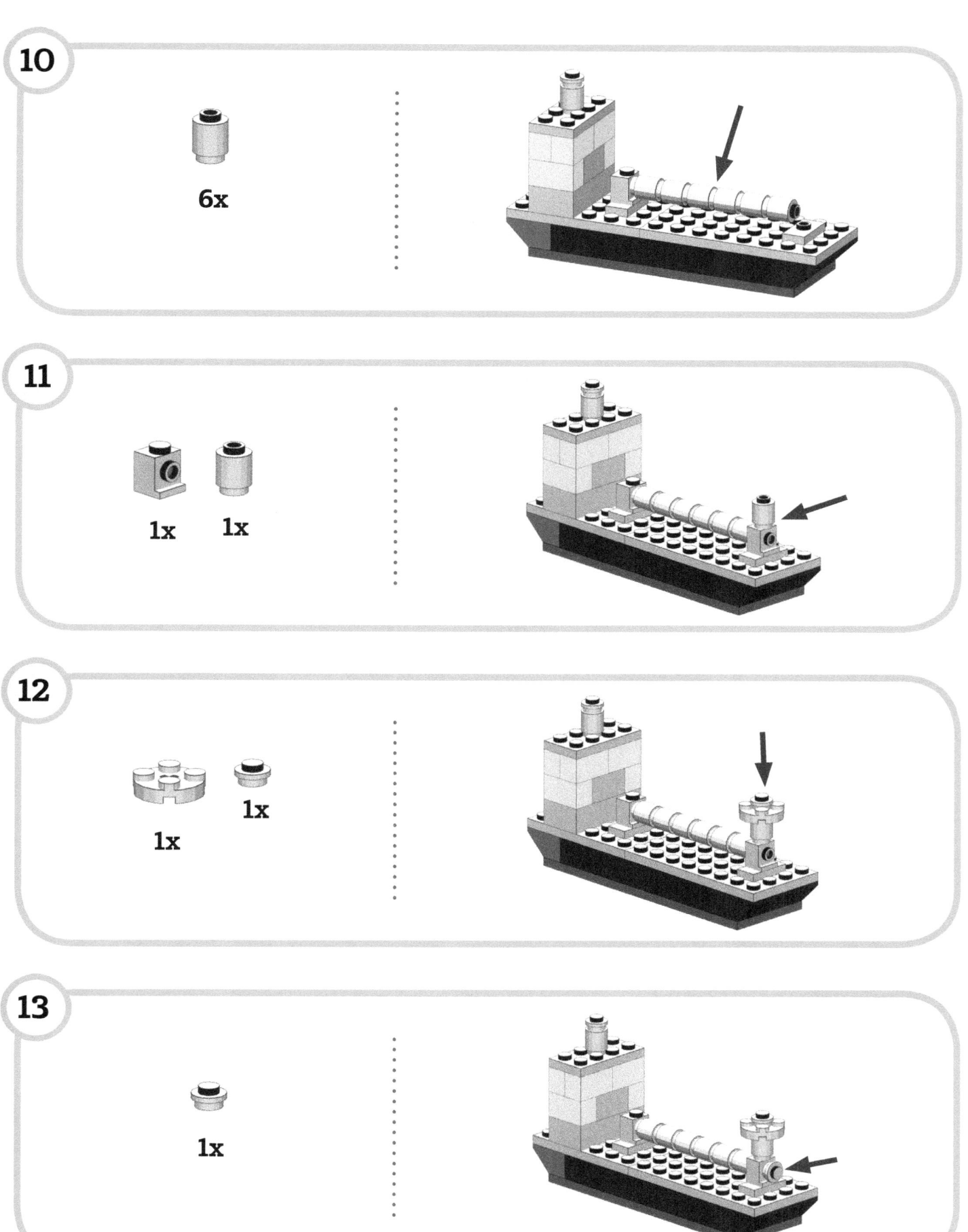

11

1x 1x

12

1x 1x

13

1x

Build a Canoe

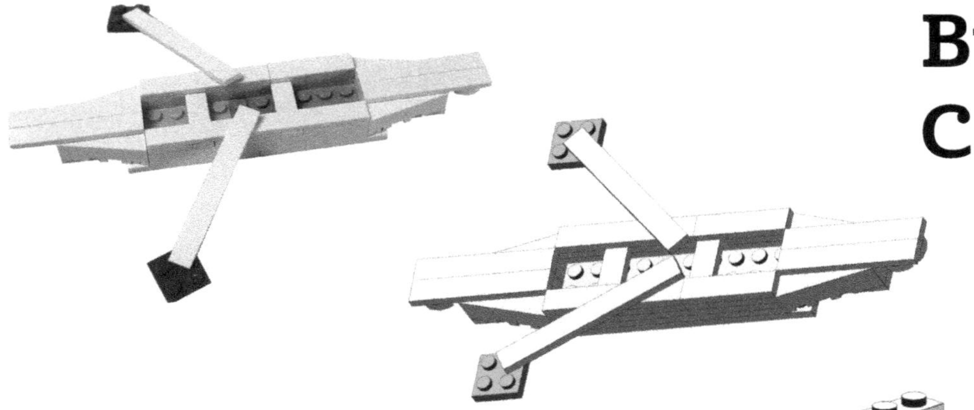

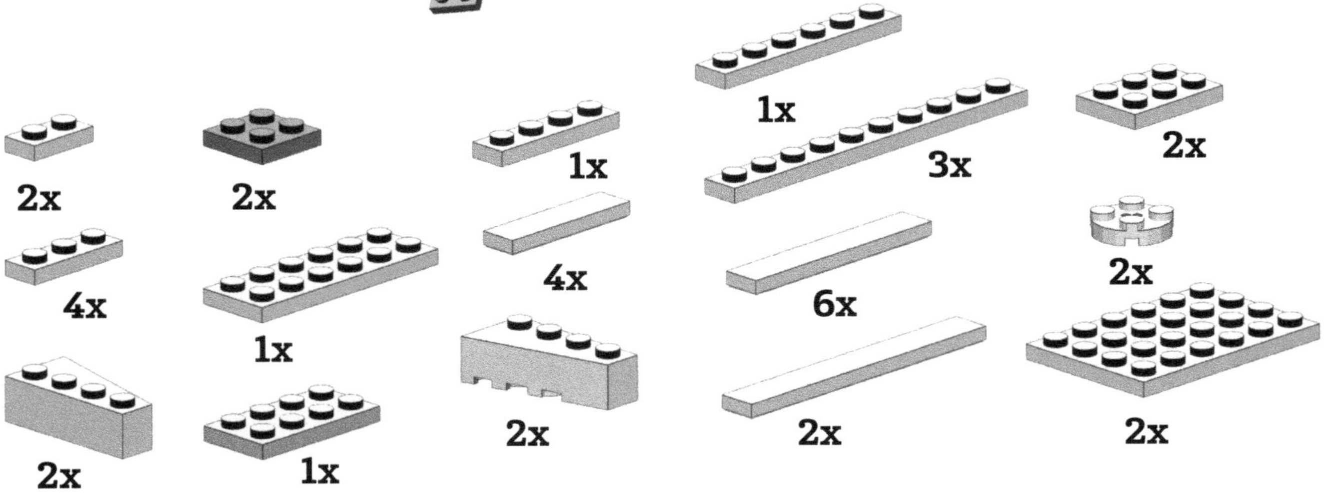

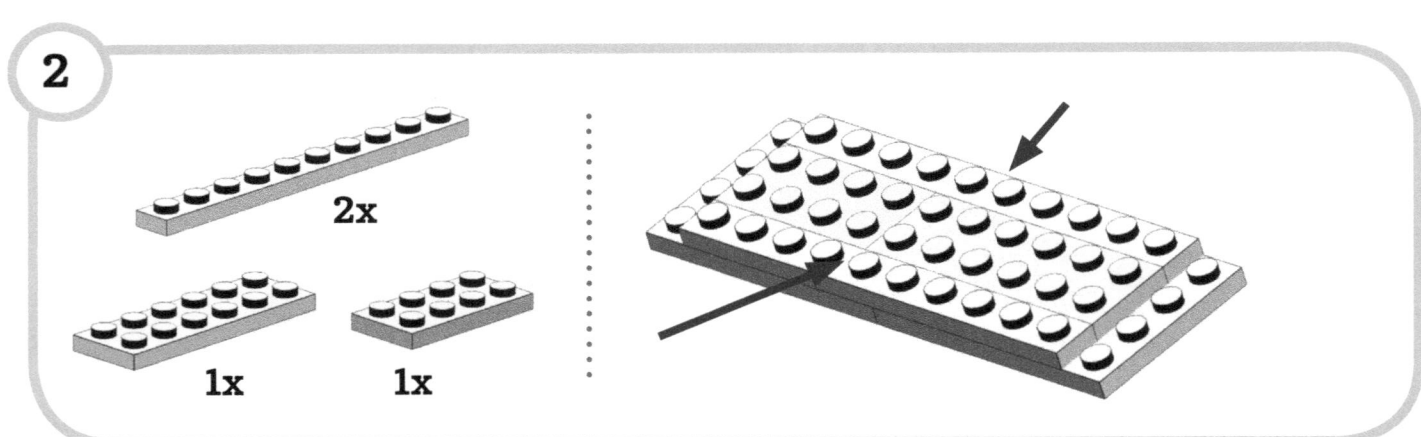

2x 2x 1x 1x 3x 2x

4x 1x 4x 6x 2x 2x

2x 1x 2x 2x 2x

1

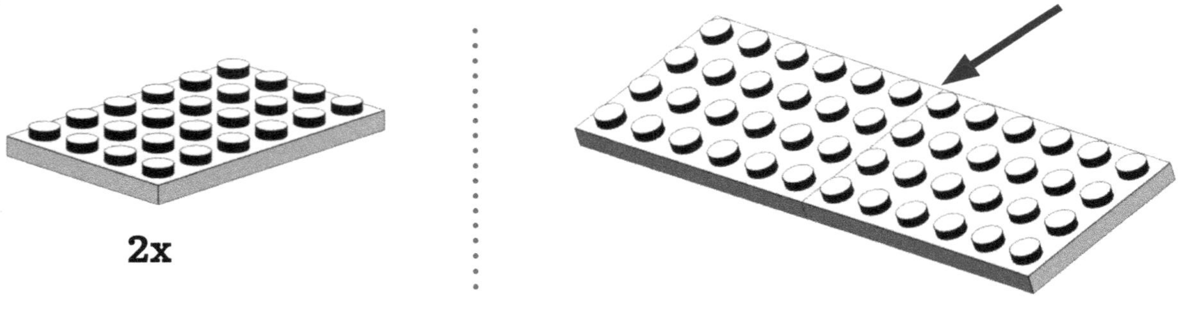

2x

2

2x

1x 1x

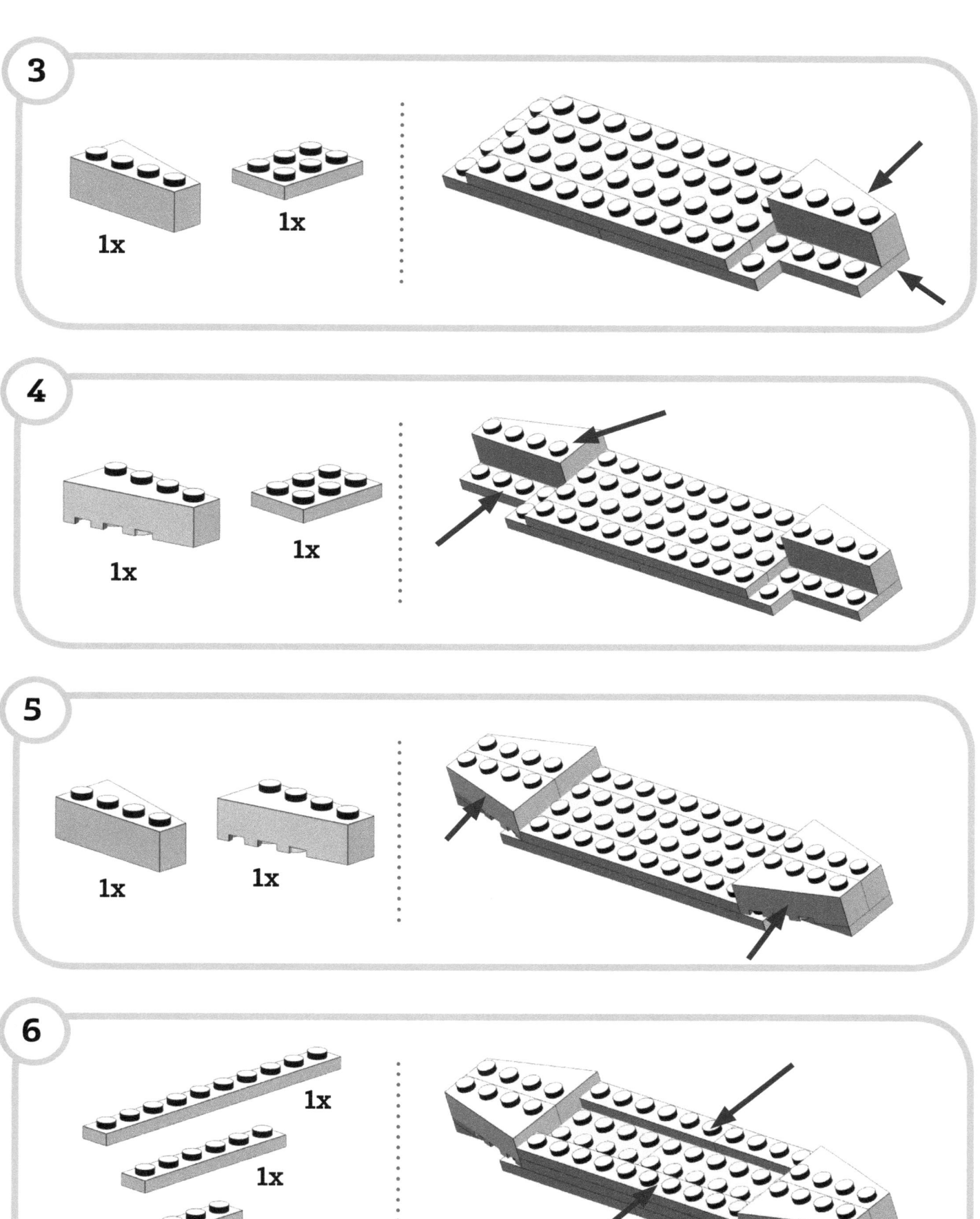

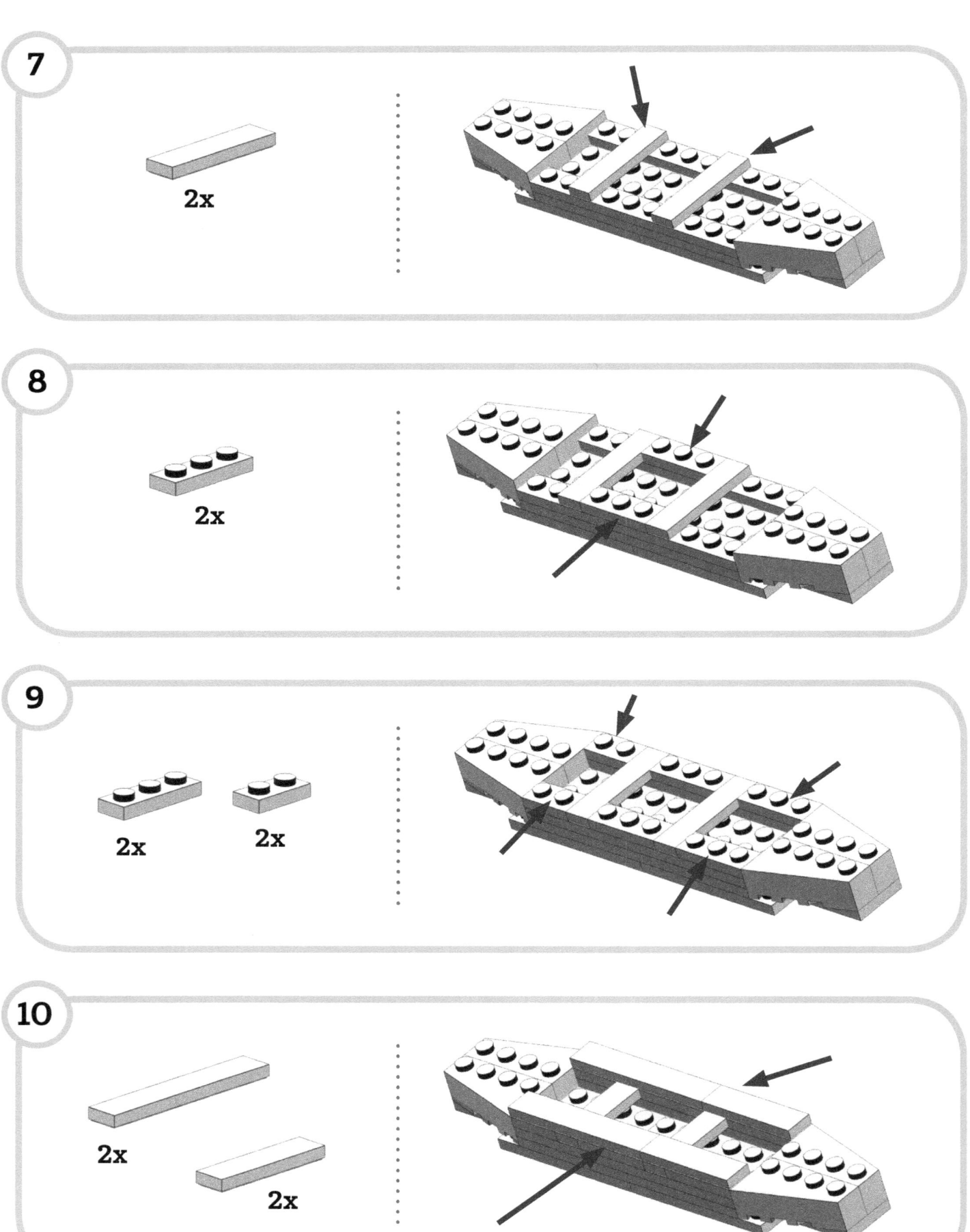

7 2x

8 2x

9 2x 2x

10 2x 2x

11

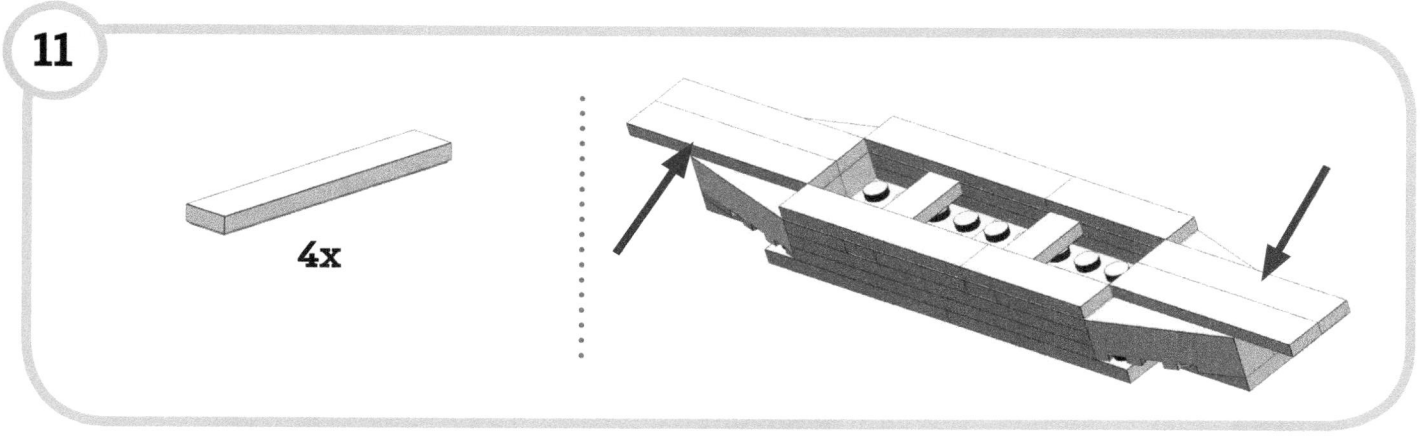

4x

12

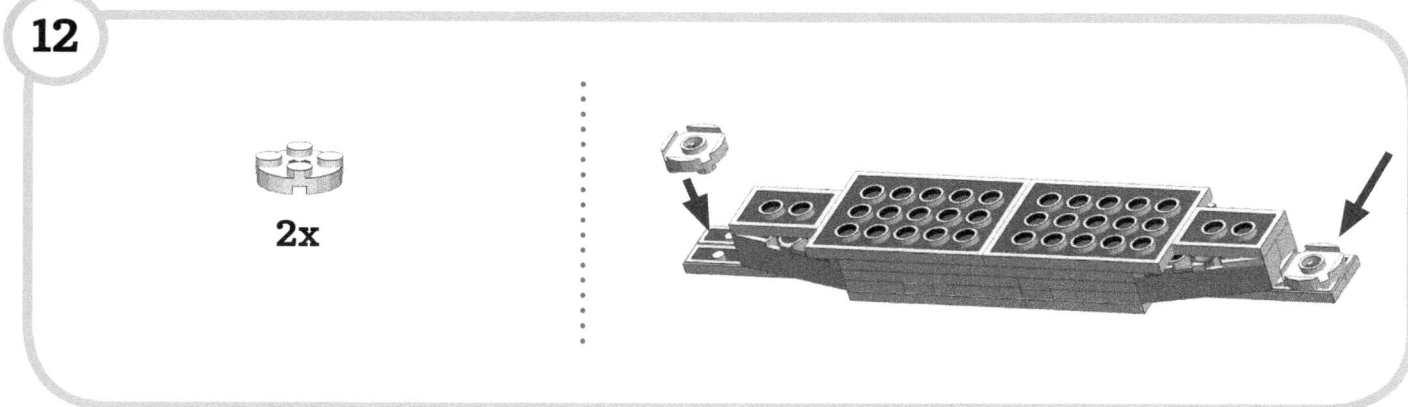

2x

13

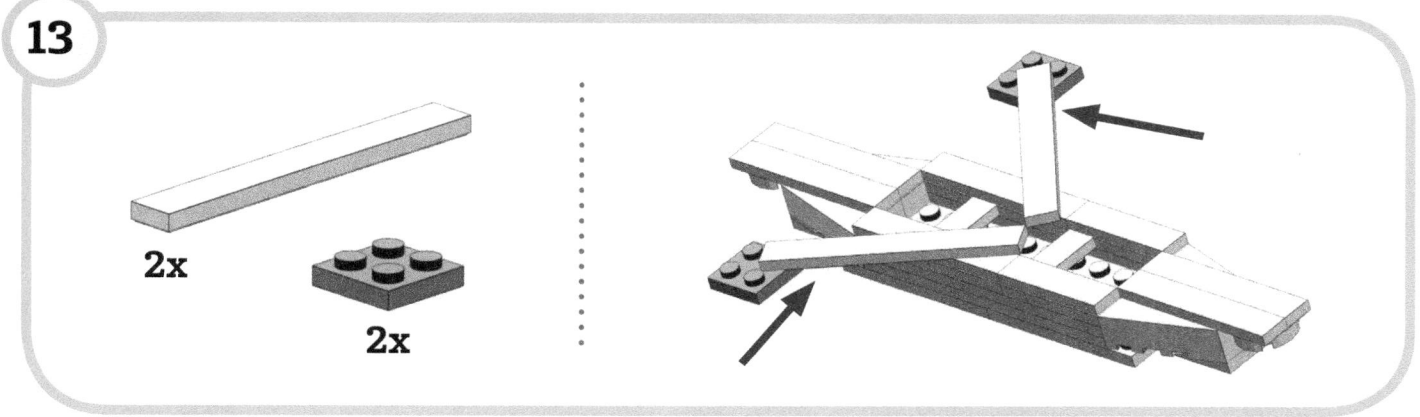

2x

2x

Build a Pontoon

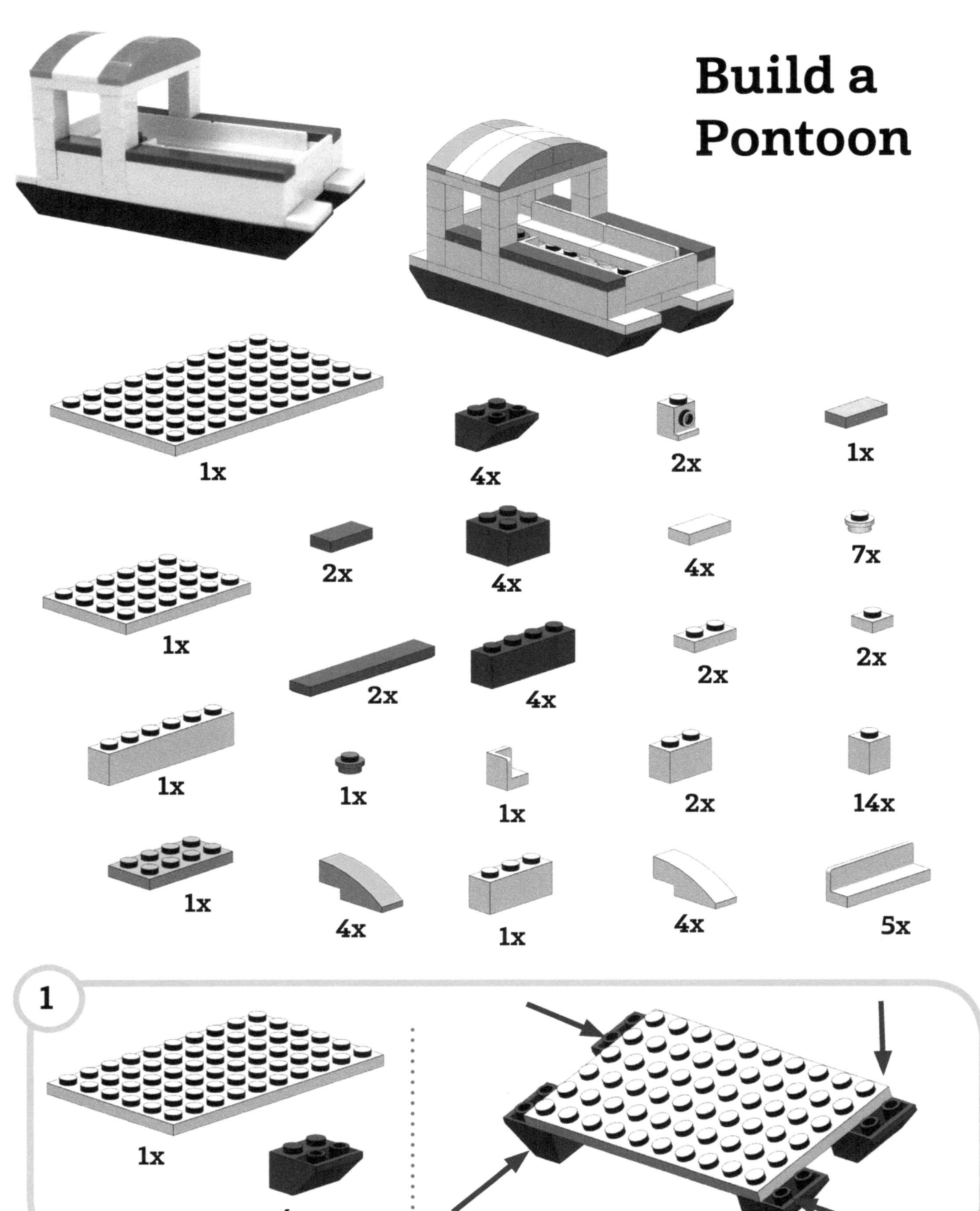

1x

4x

2x

1x

2x

4x

4x

7x

1x

2x

2x

2x

4x

14x

1x

1x

1x

2x

1x

1x

4x

1x

4x

5x

1

1x

4x

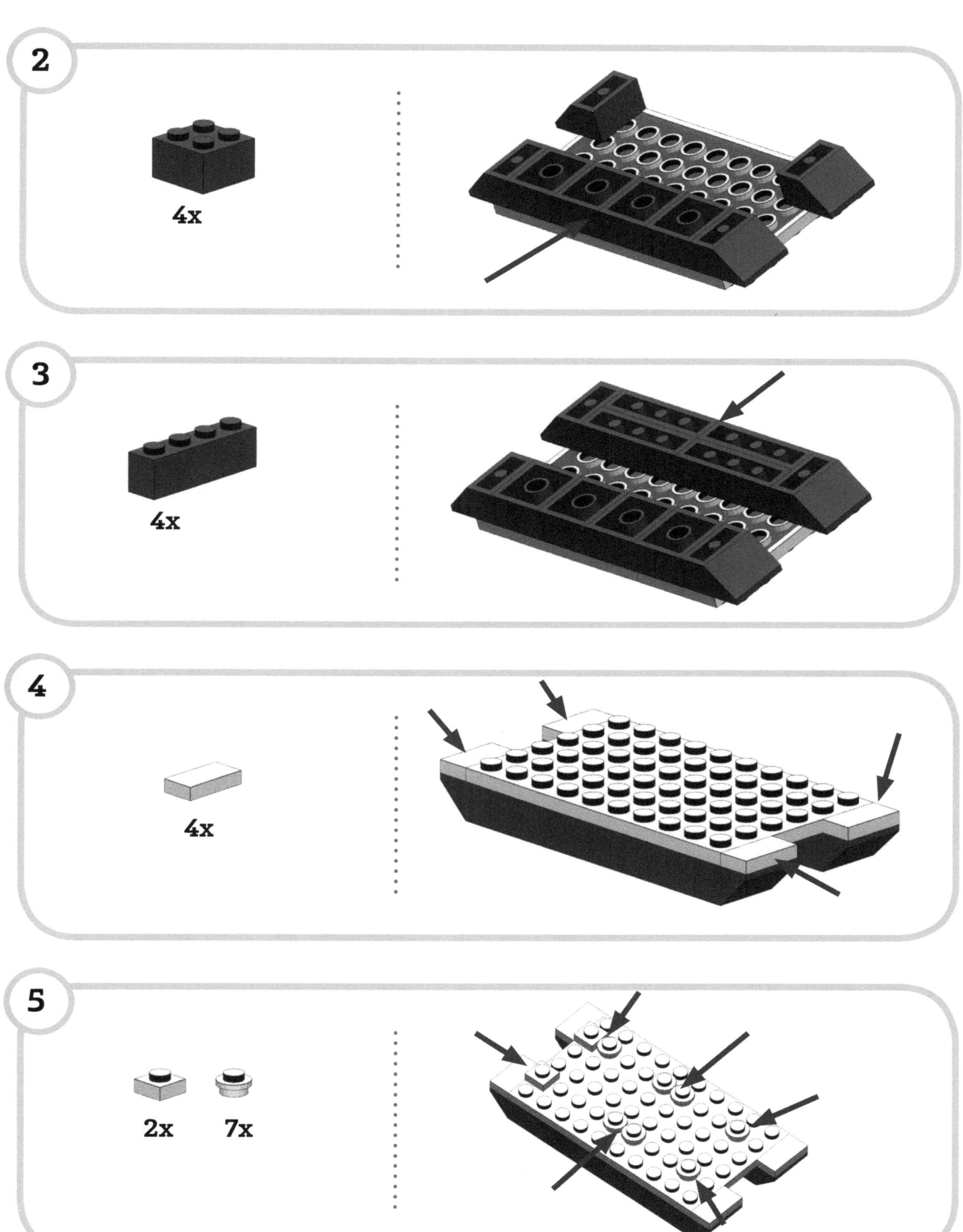

2 4x

3 4x

4 4x

5 2x 7x

6

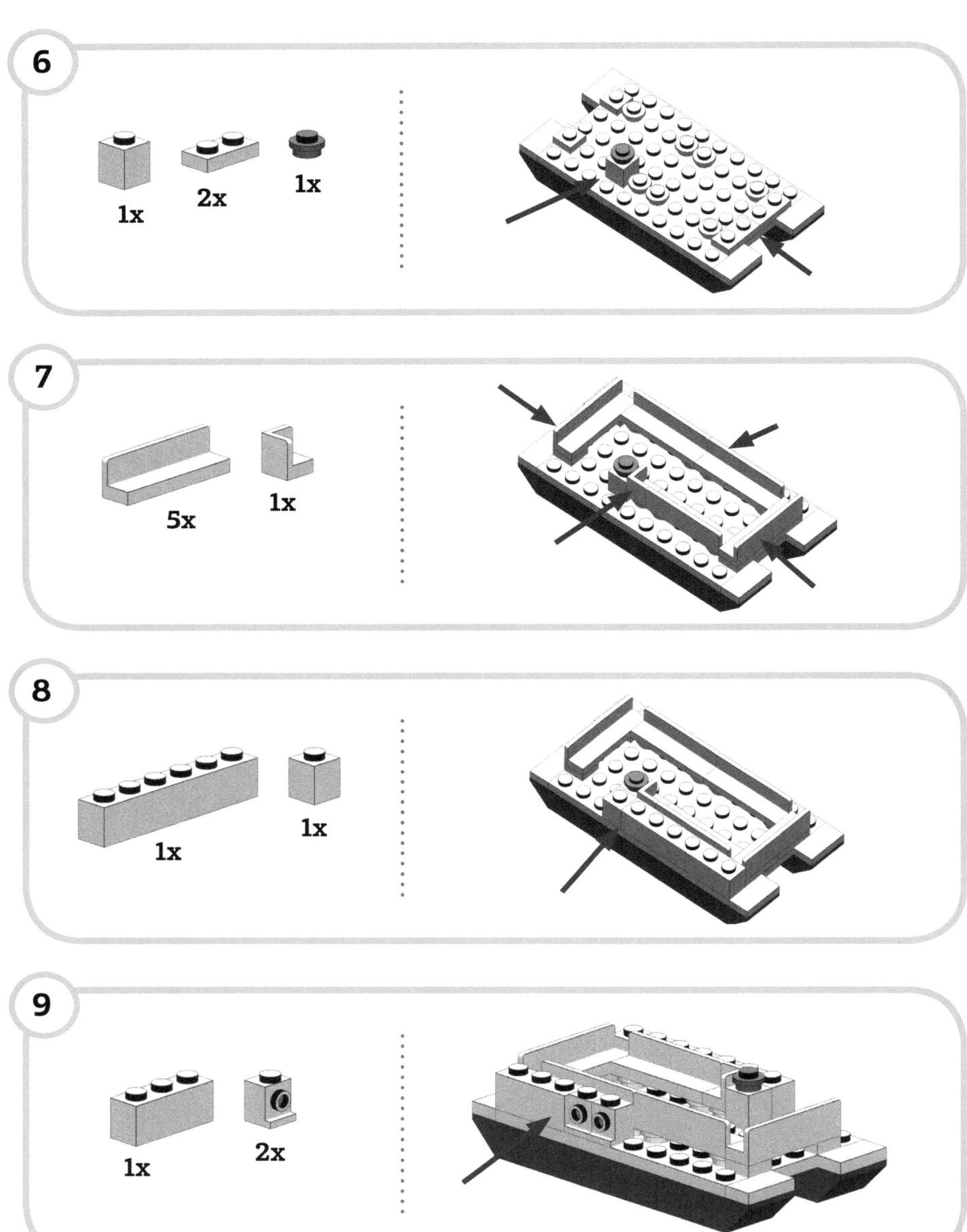

1x 2x 1x

7

5x 1x

8

1x 1x

9

1x 2x

10

2x 4x

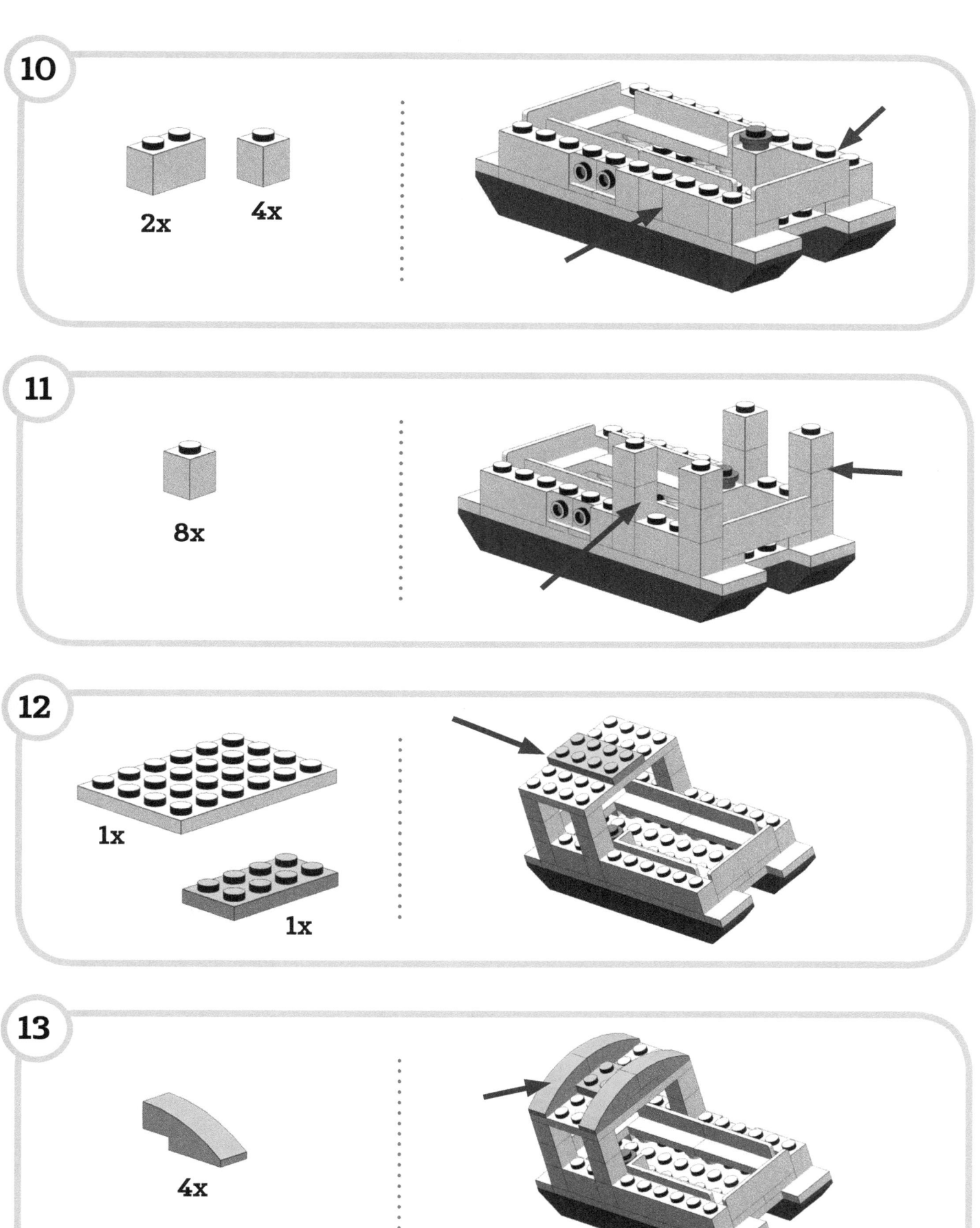

11

8x

12

1x

1x

13

4x

14

4x

15

2x **2x**

16

1x

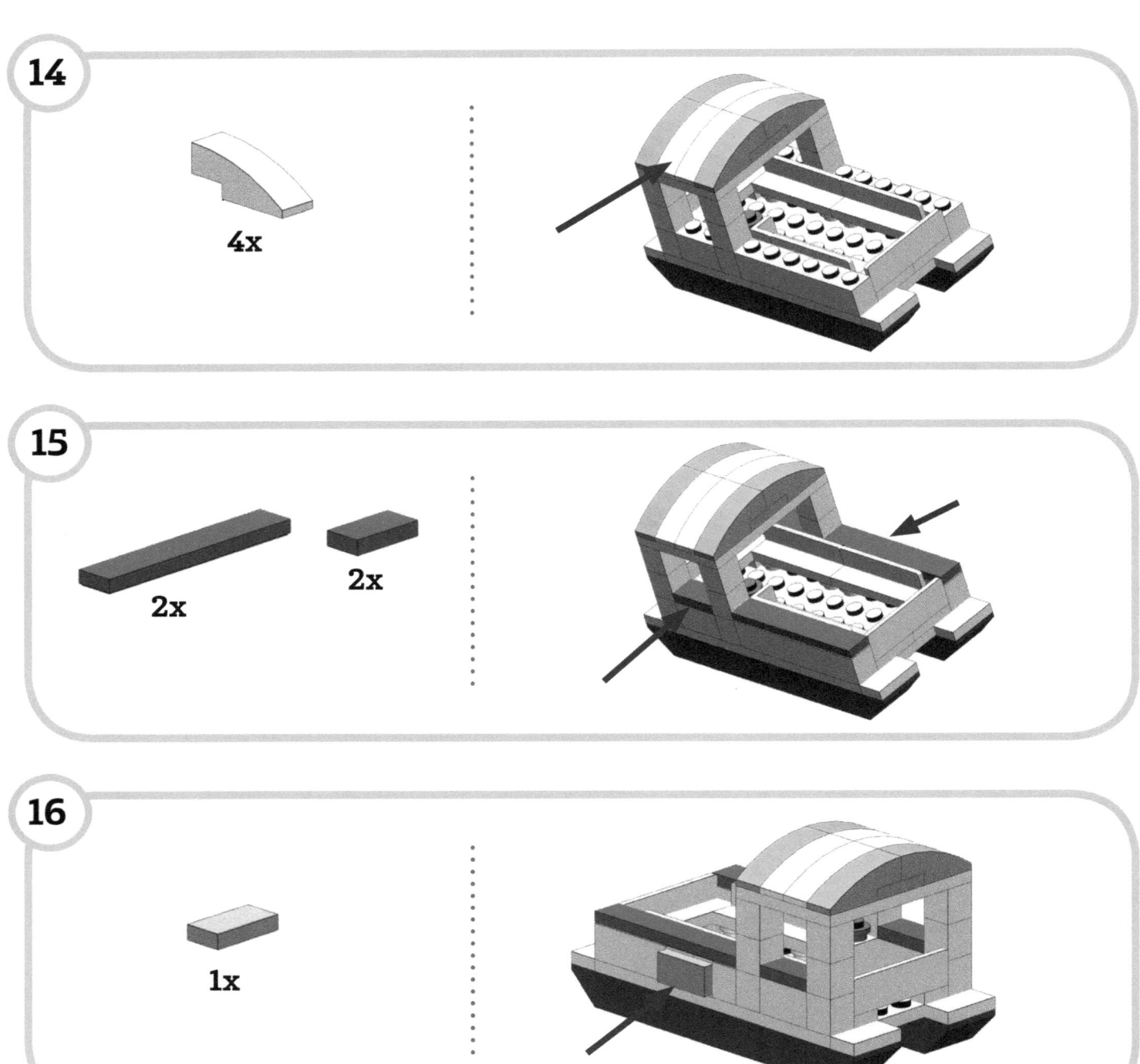

Build a Kayak

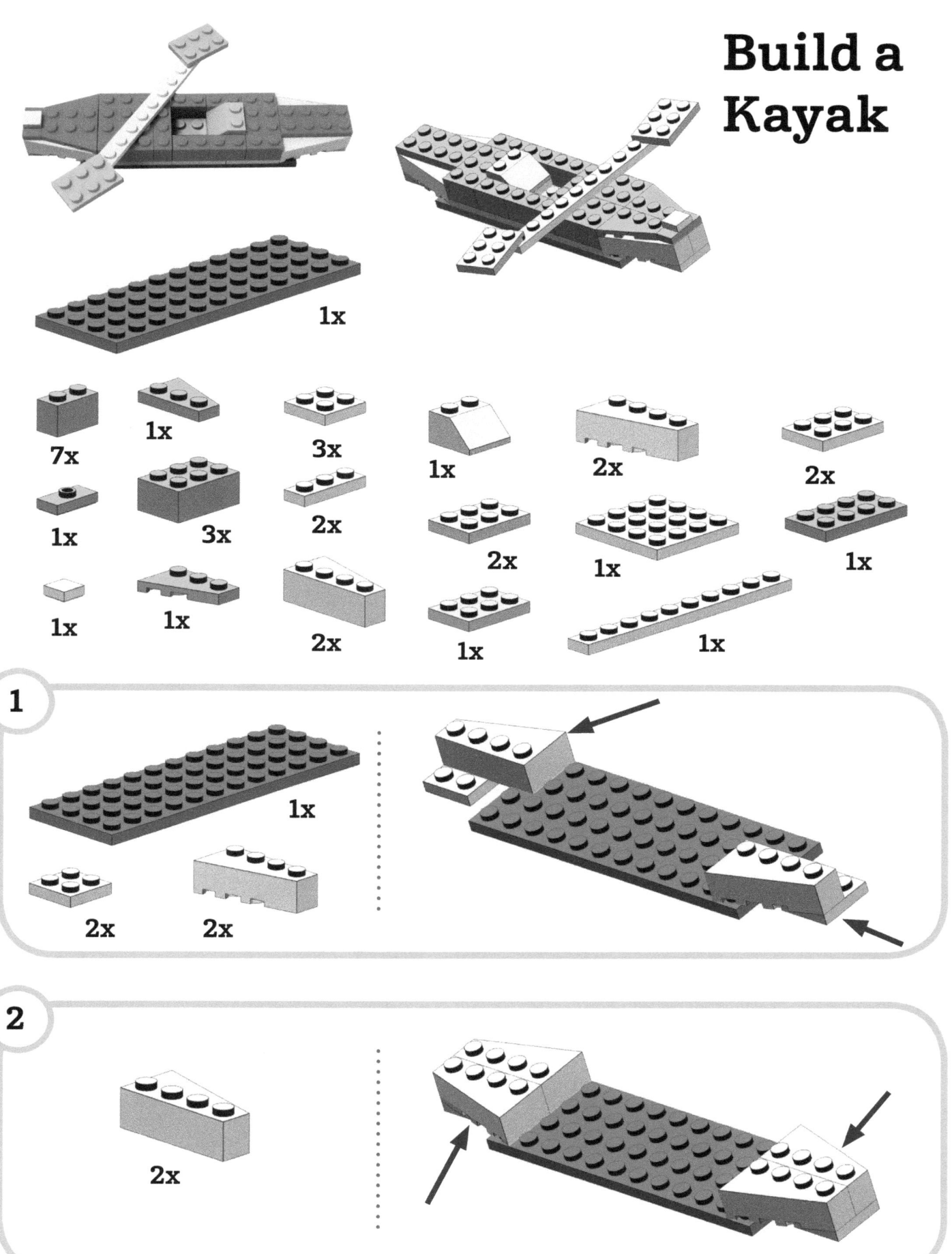

1x

7x 1x 3x 1x 2x 2x

1x 3x 2x 2x 1x 1x

1x 1x 2x 1x 1x

1

1x

2x 2x

2

2x

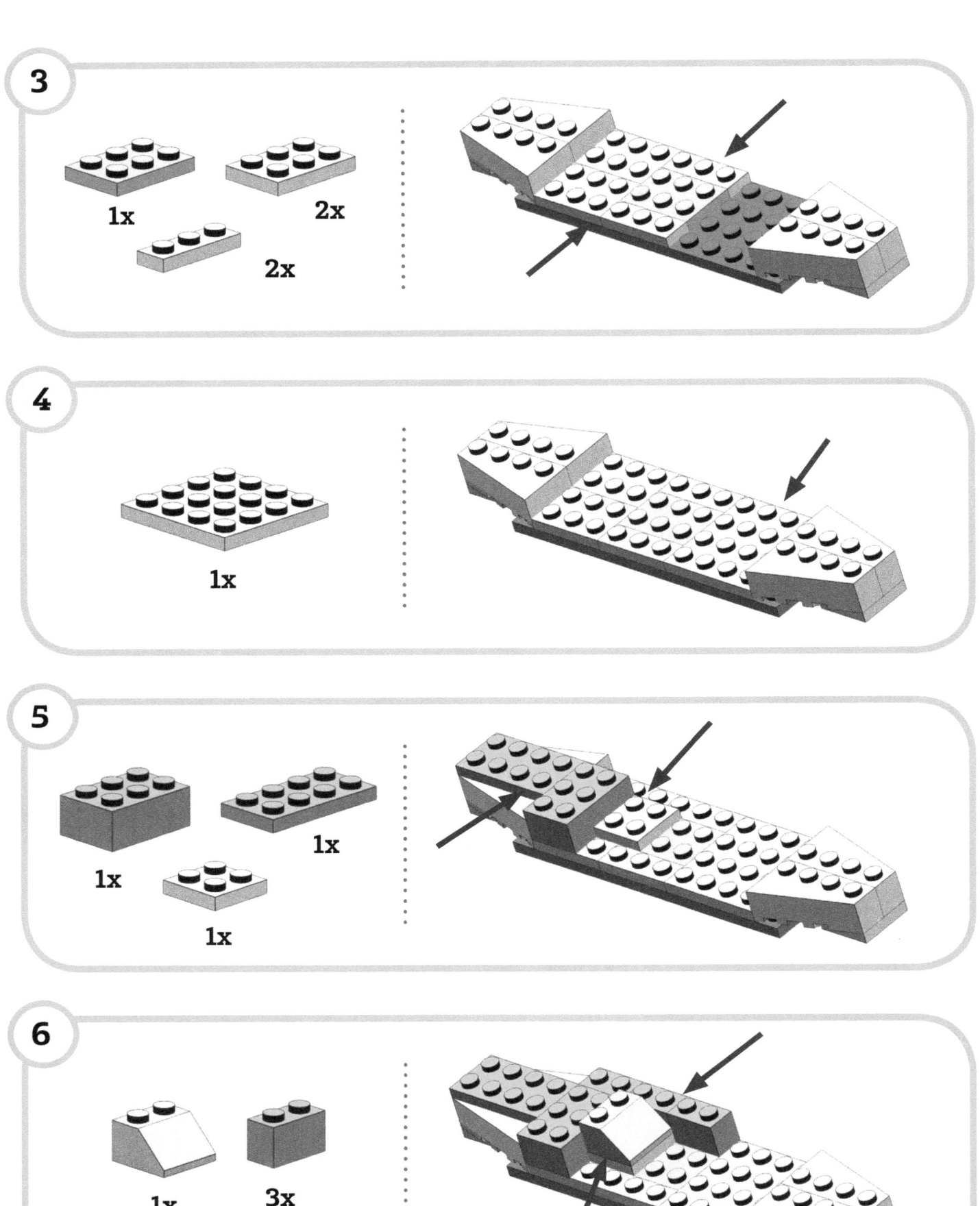

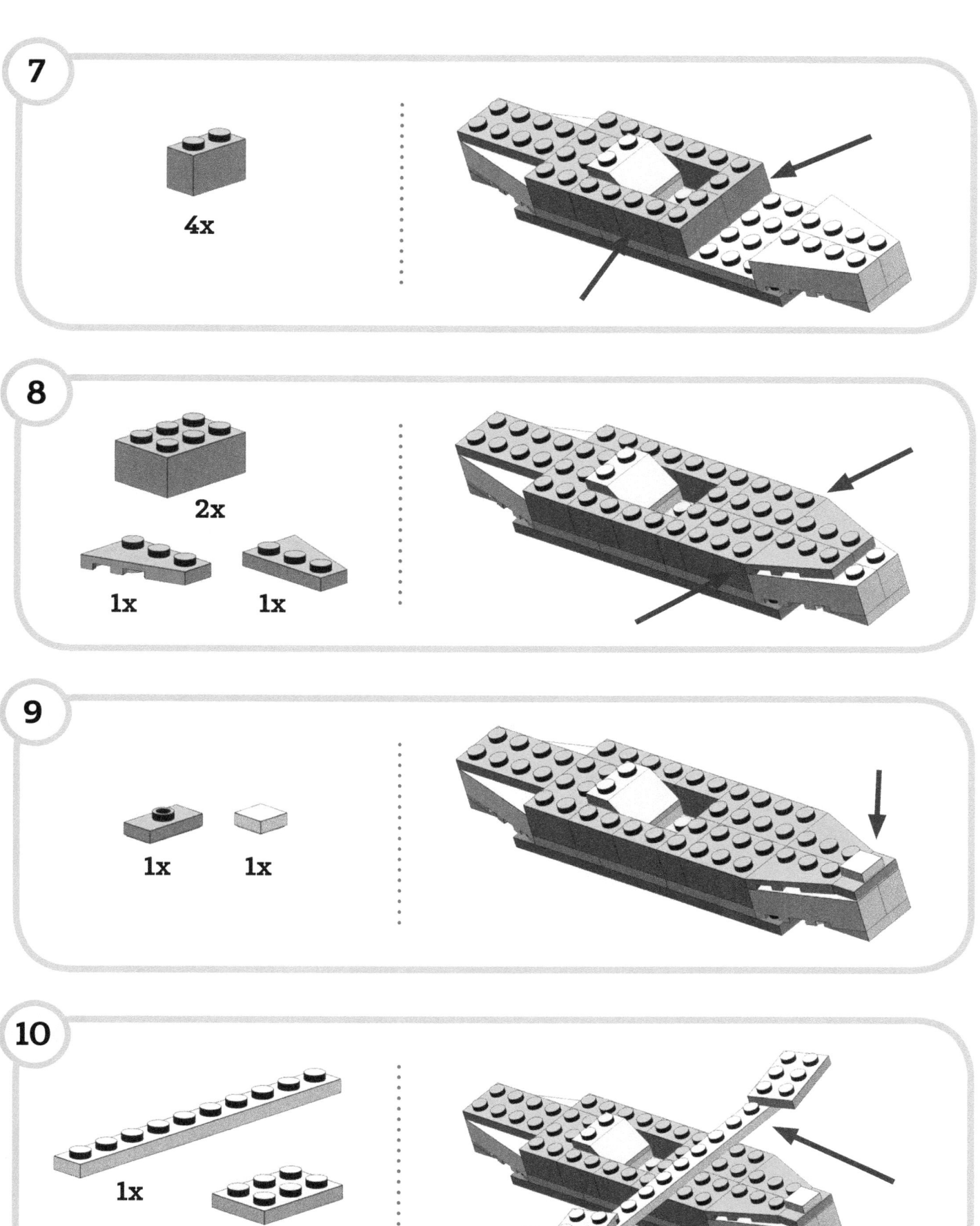

Build a Trimaran

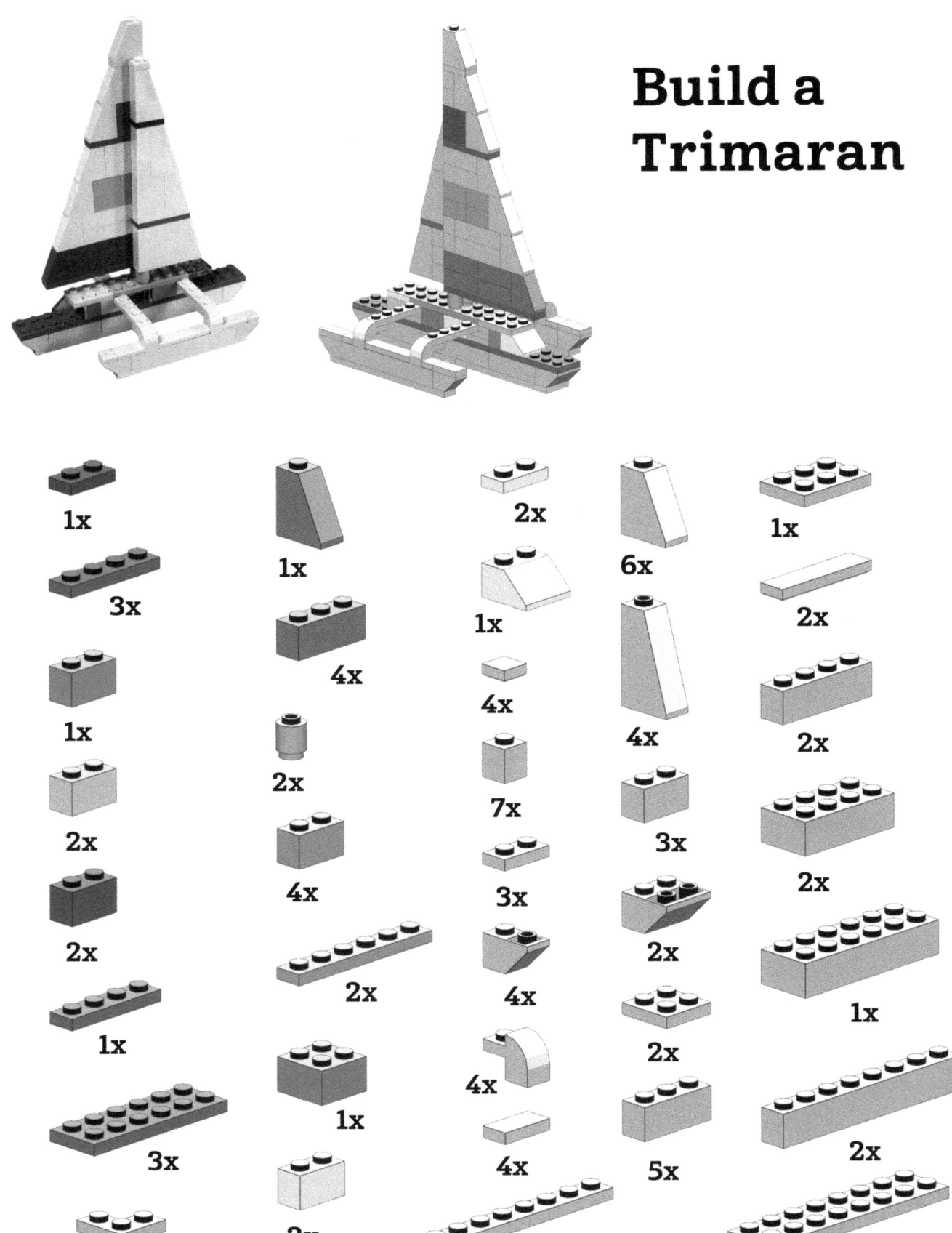

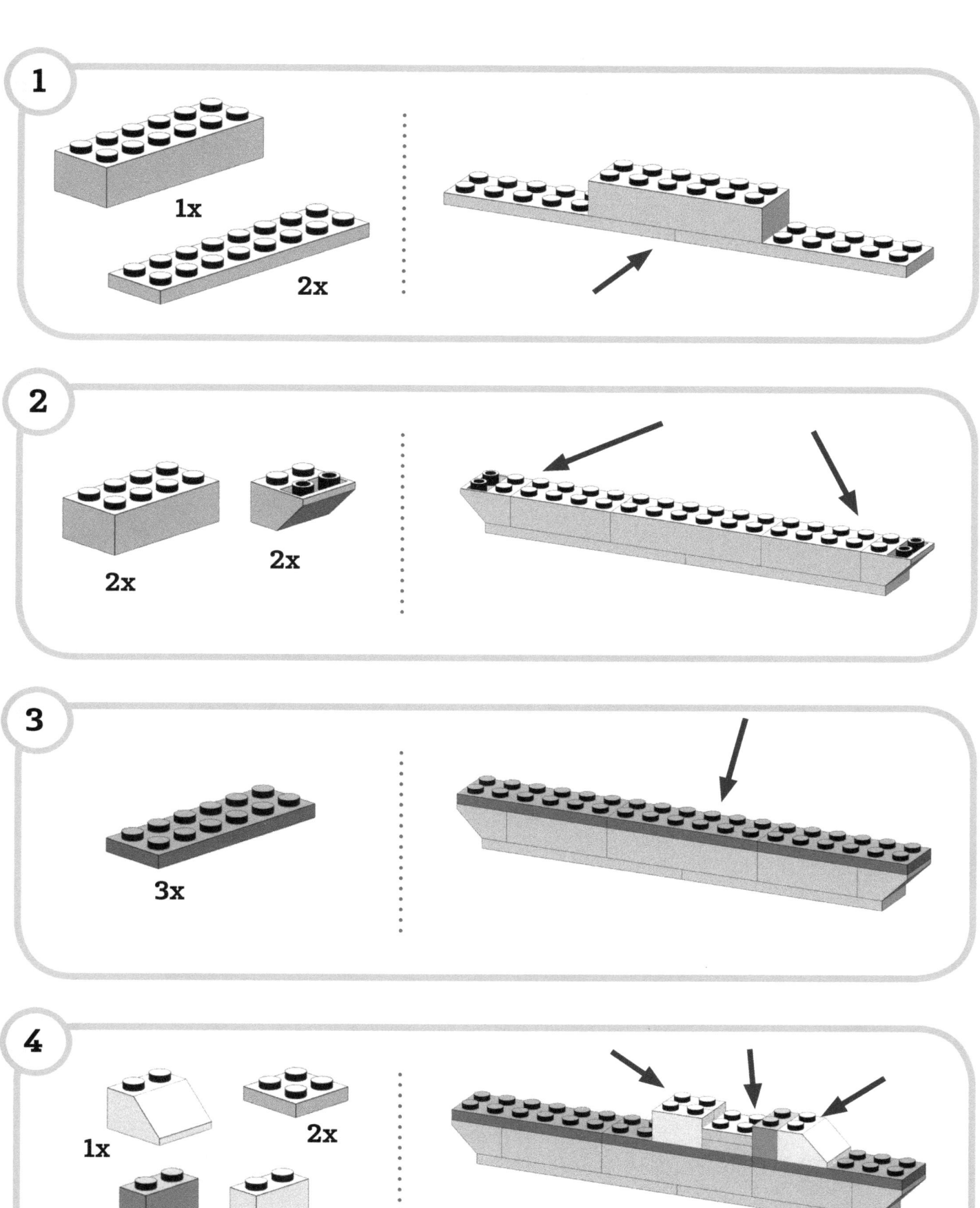

1

1x

2x

2

2x

2x

3

3x

4

1x

2x

1x

2x

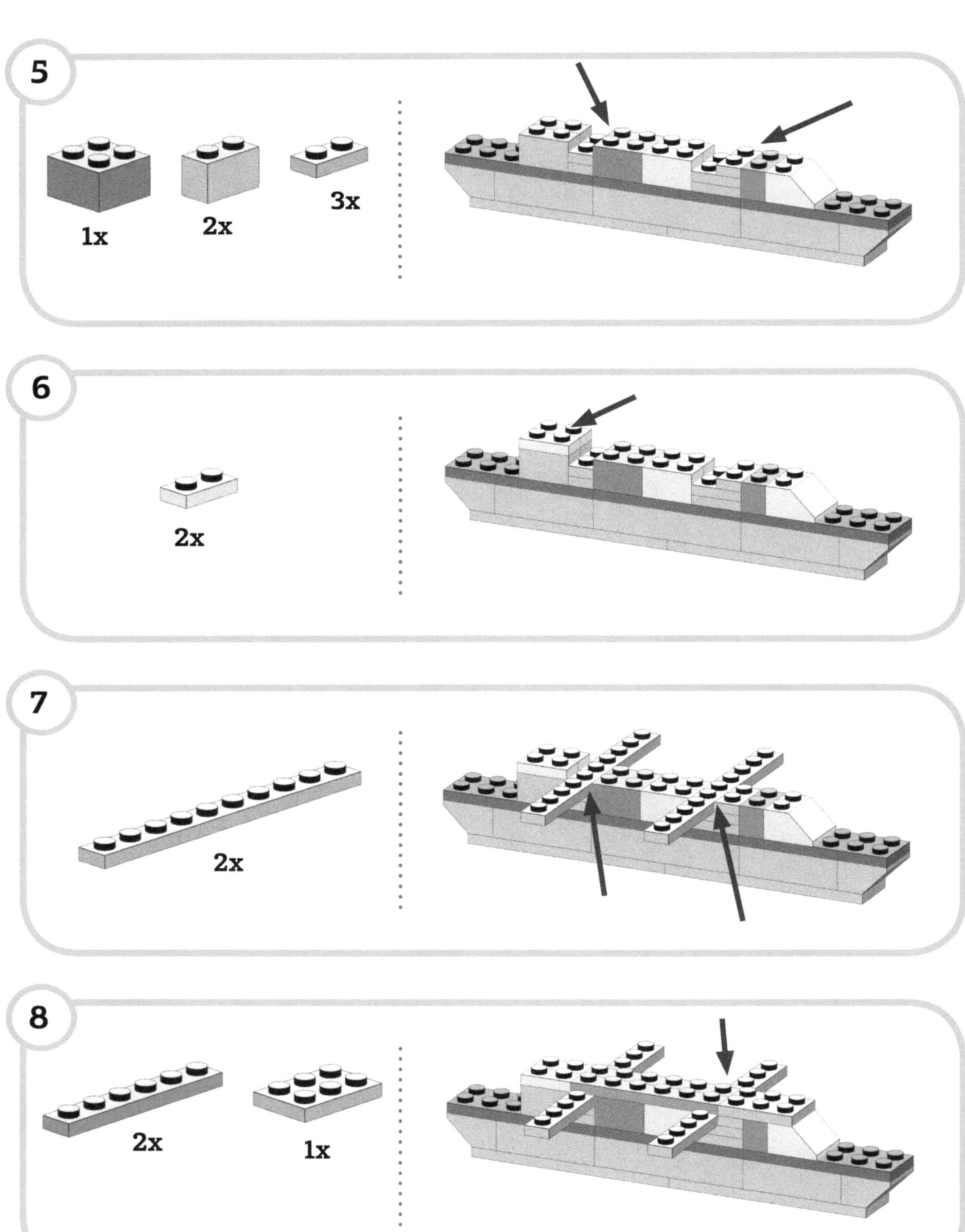

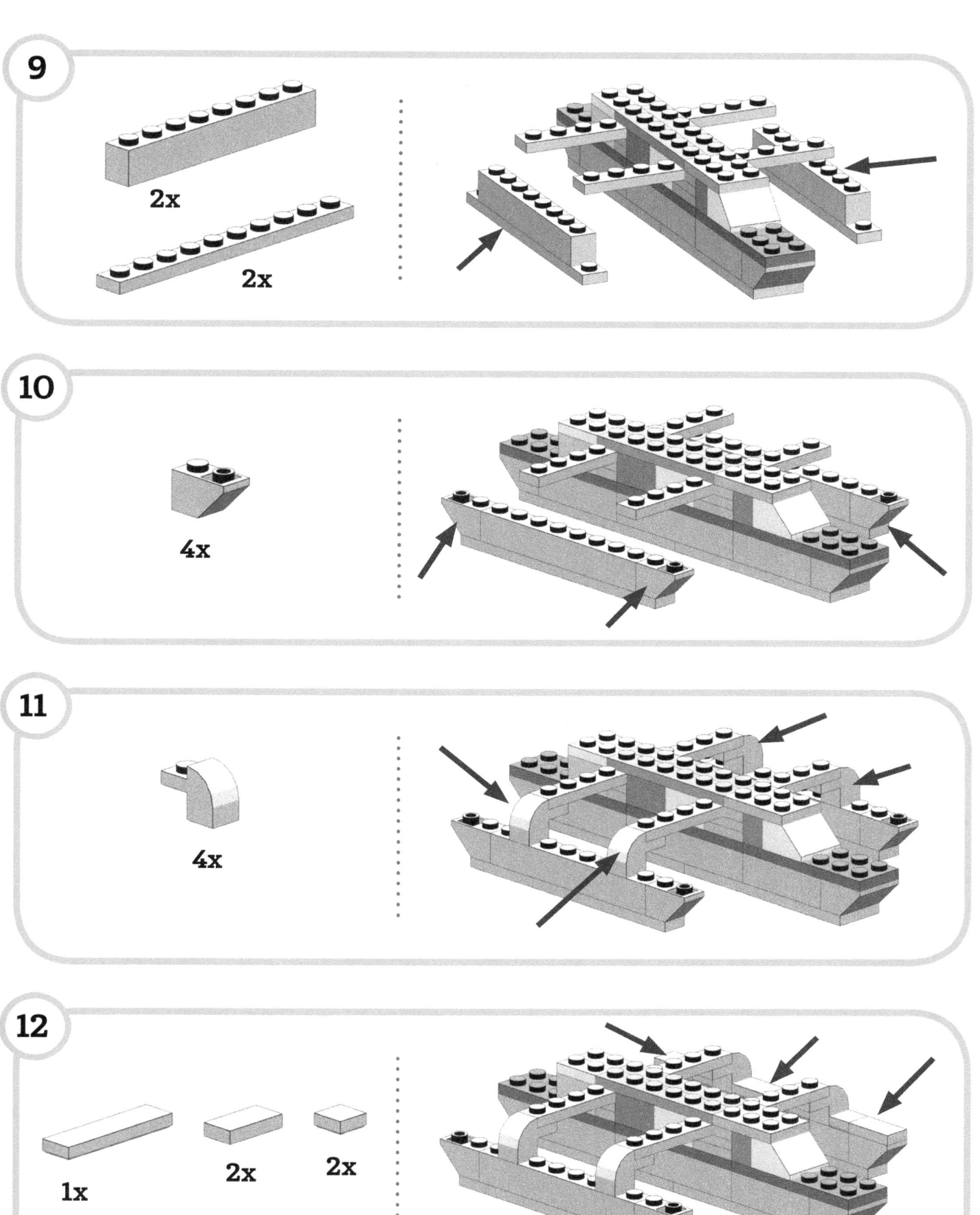

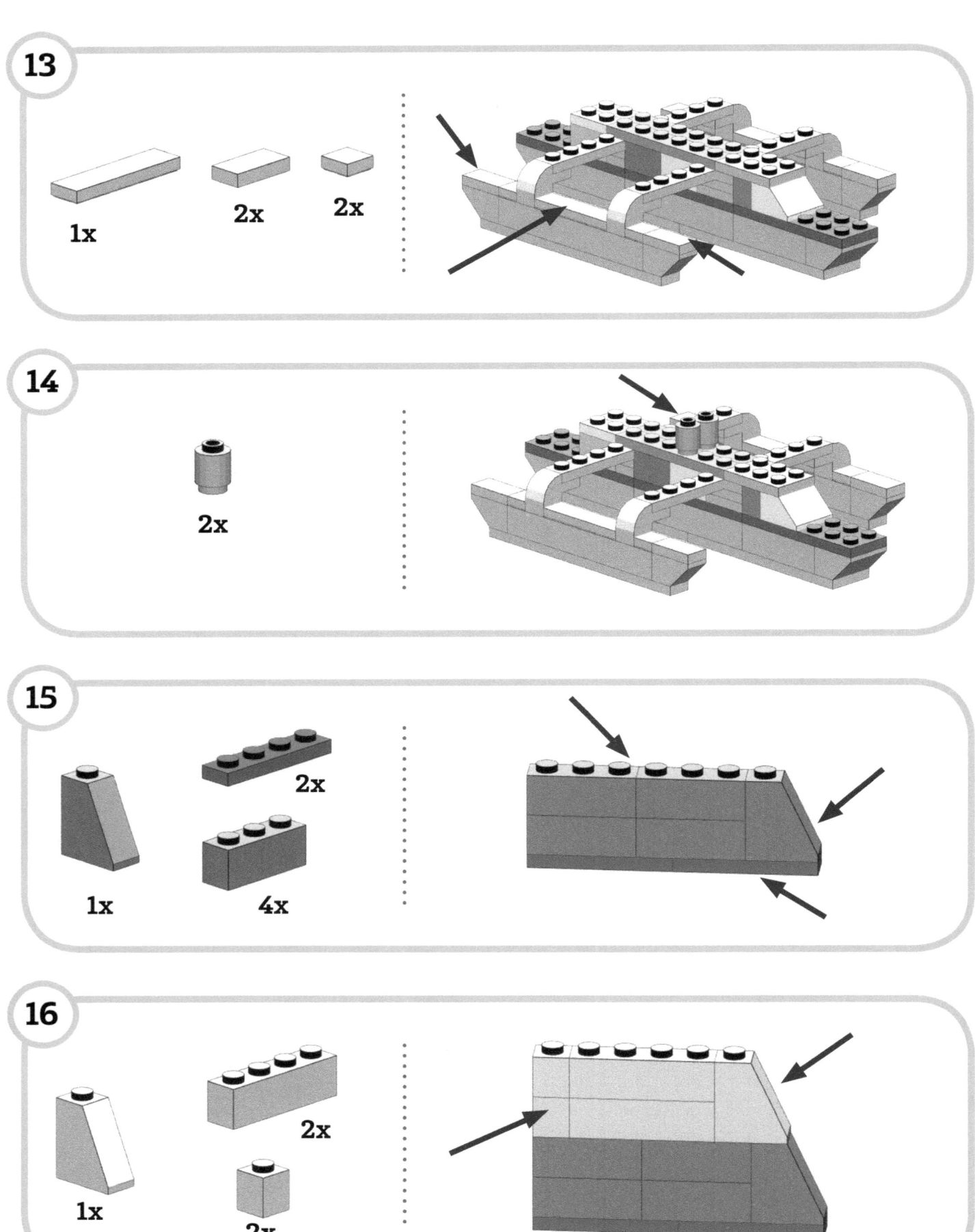

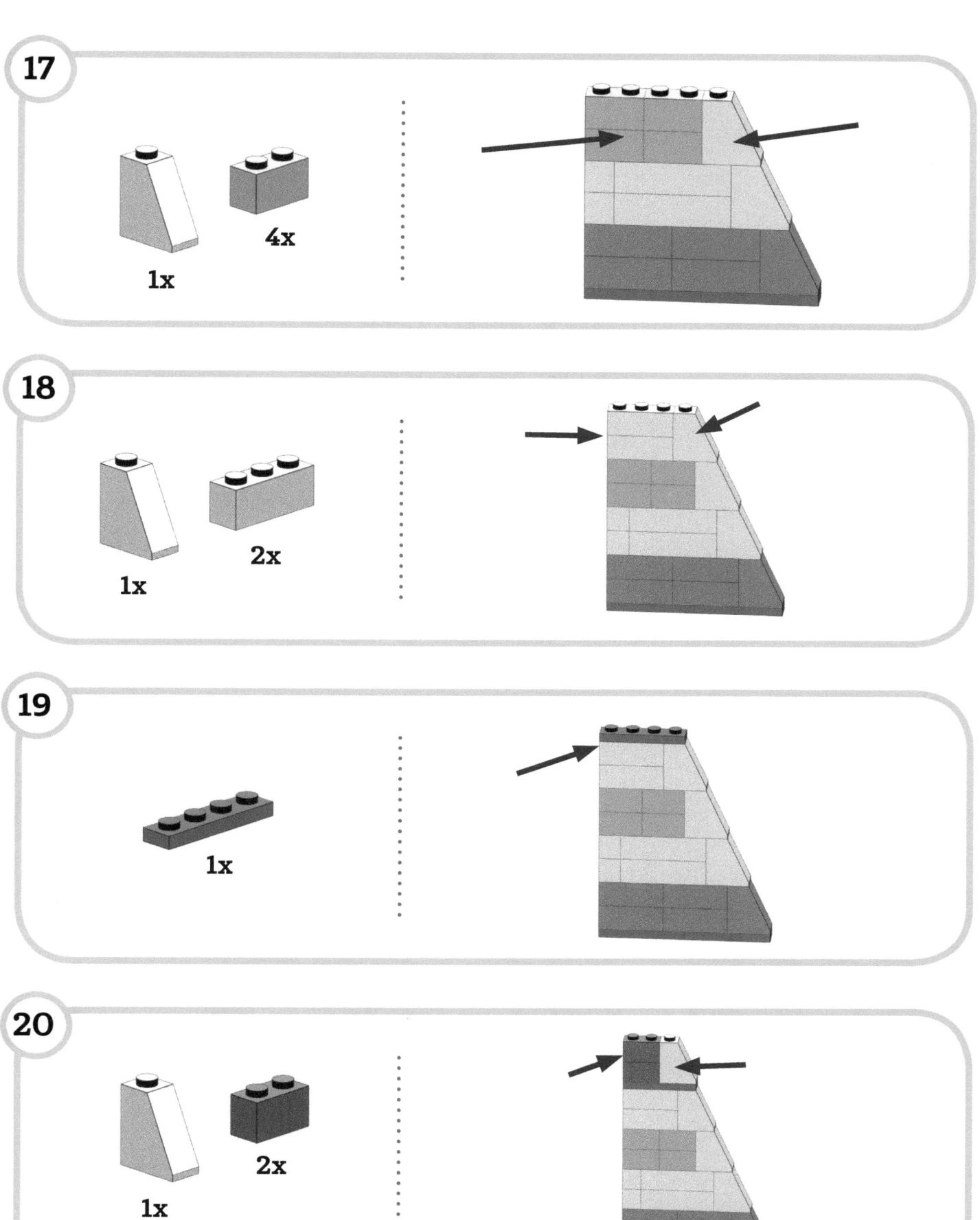

17 1x 4x

18 1x 2x

19 1x

20 1x 2x

21

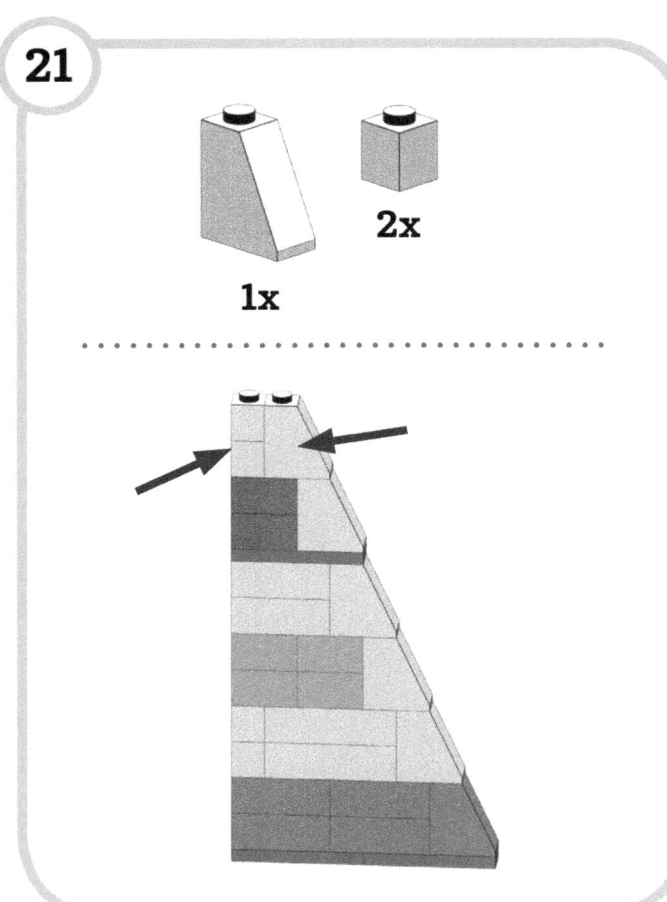

1x 2x

22

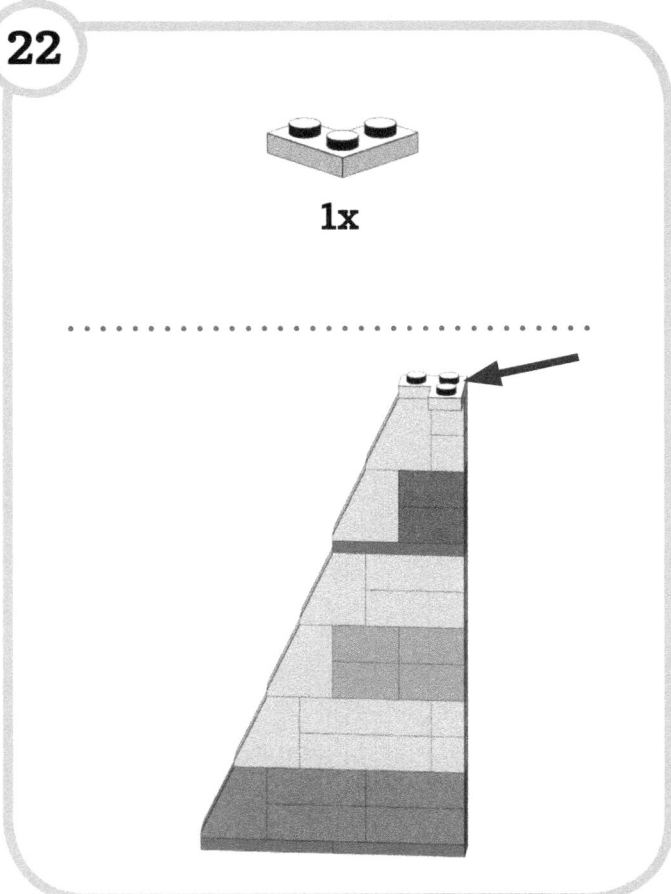

1x

23

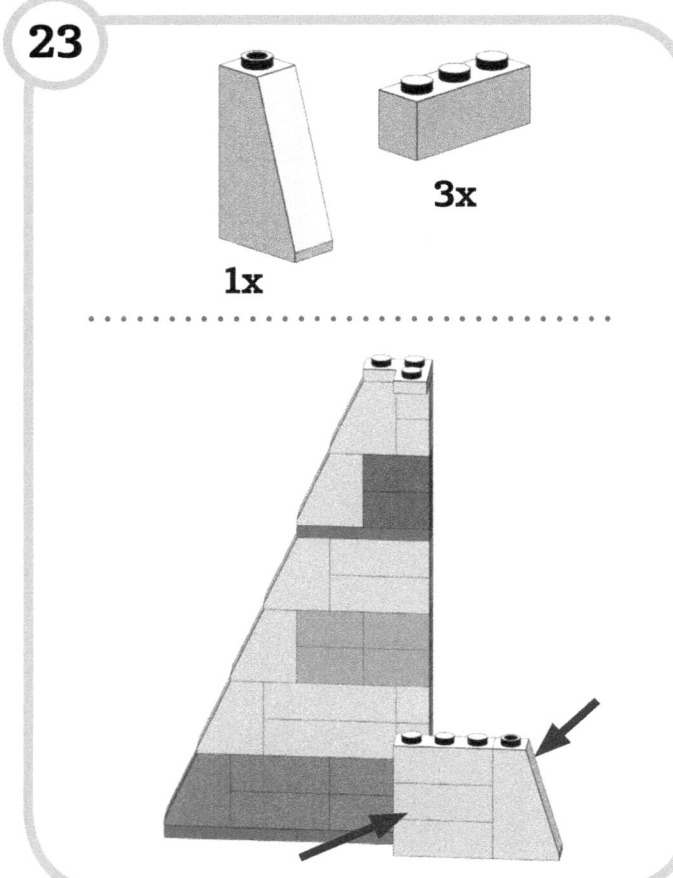

1x 3x

24

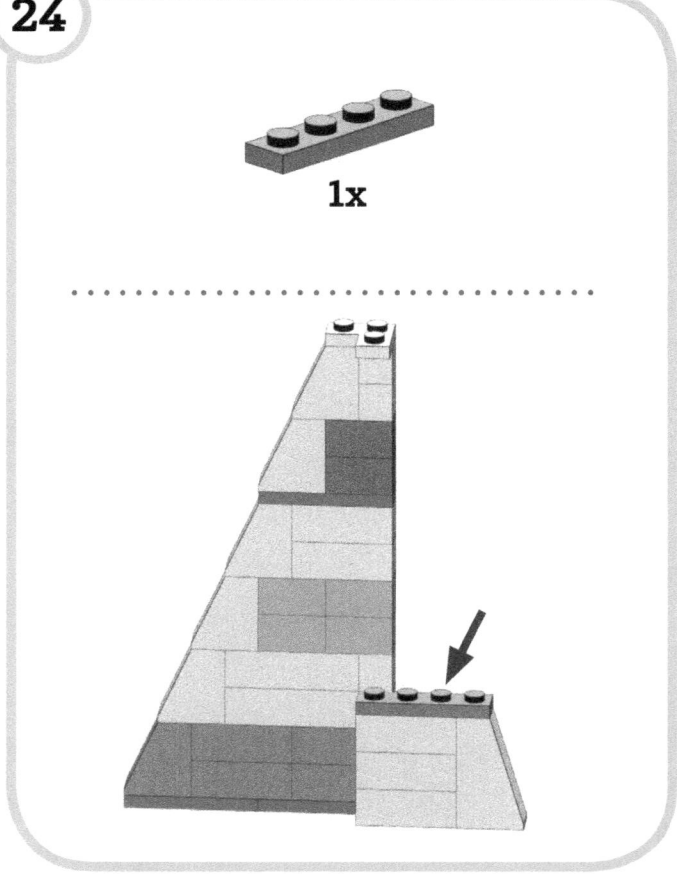

1x

25

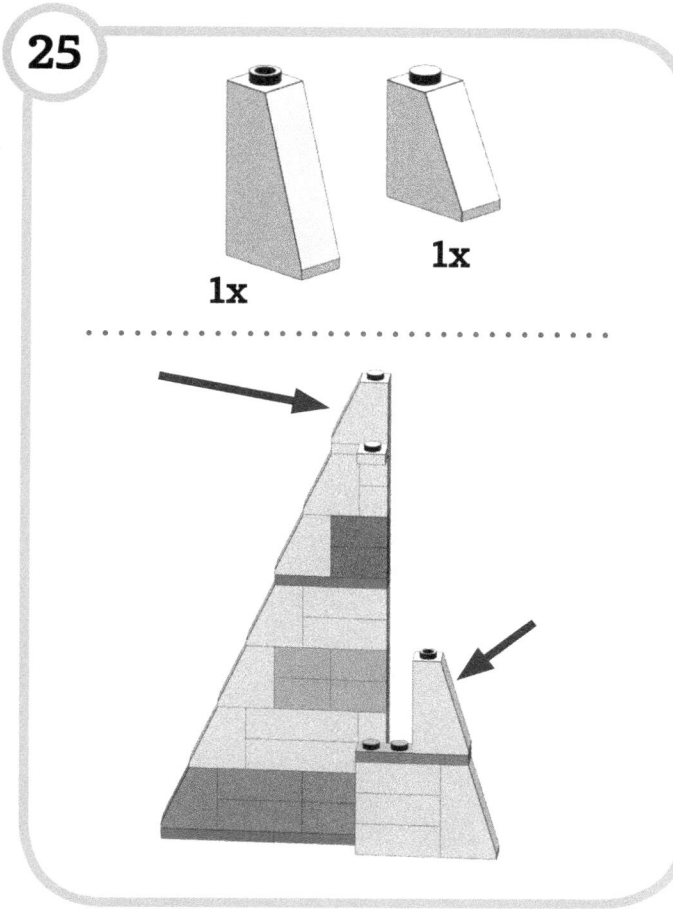

1x 1x

26

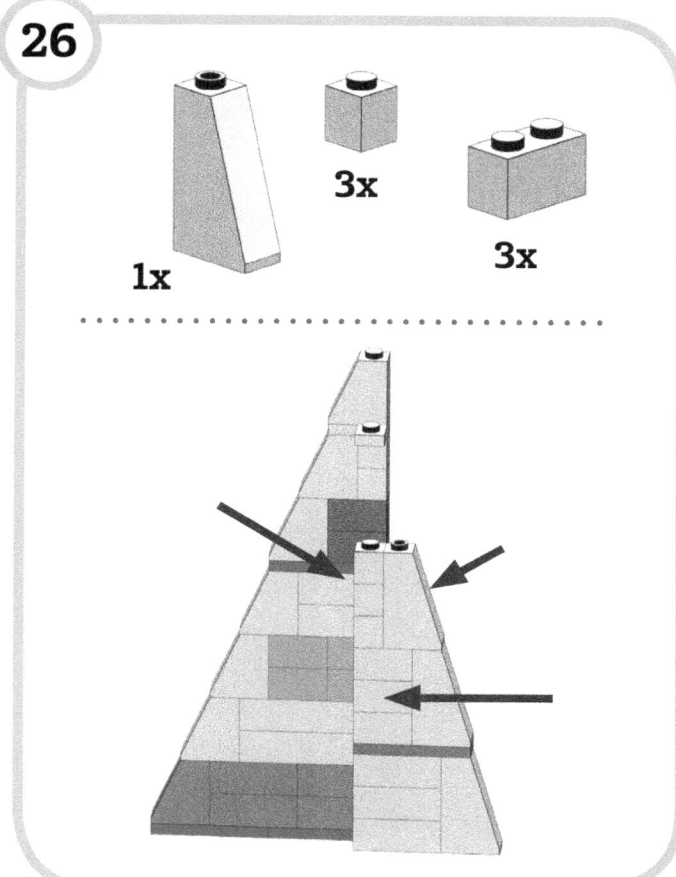

1x 3x 3x

27

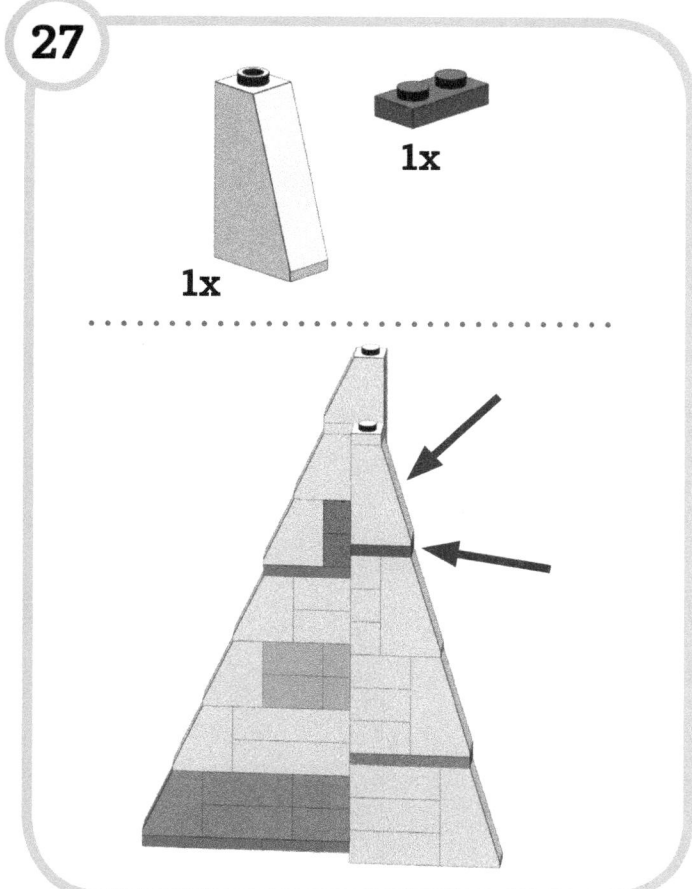

1x 1x

28

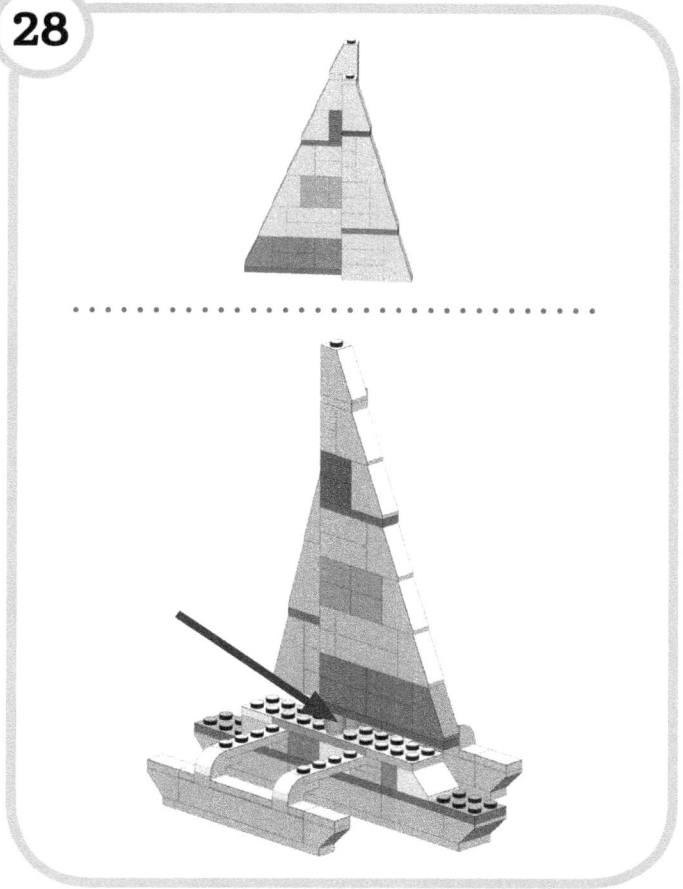

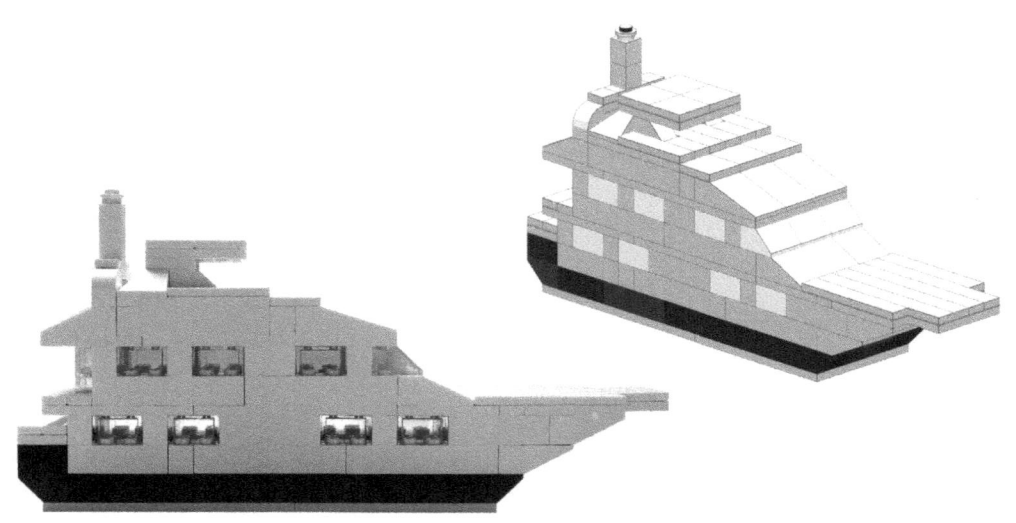

Build a Super Yacht

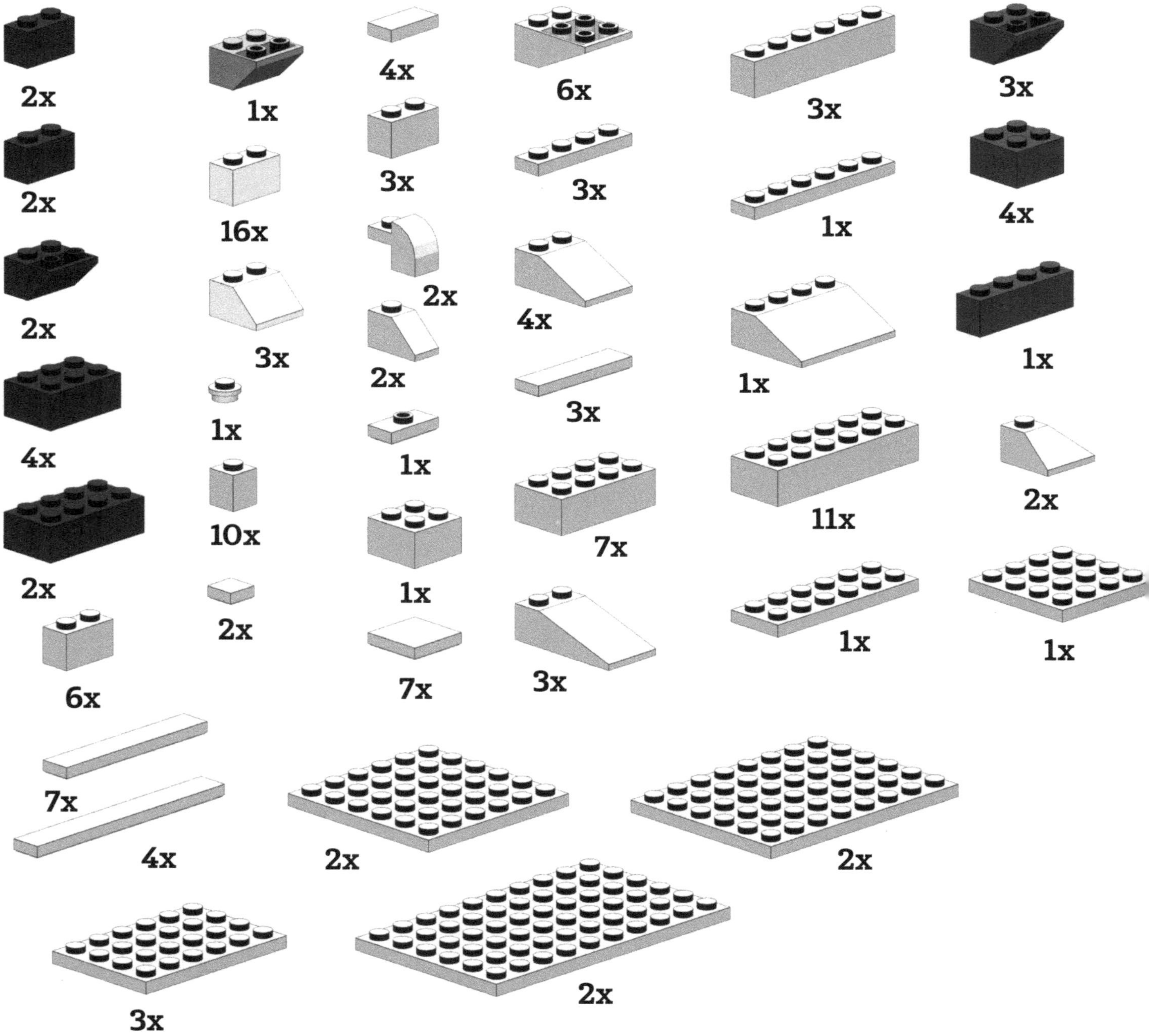

2x

1x

4x

6x

3x

3x

2x

2x

1x

16x

3x

3x

4x

1x

4x

2x

3x

2x

4x

1x

4x

1x

2x

3x

1x

2x

10x

1x

1x

11x

2x

7x

2x

1x

1x

1x

6x

7x

3x

7x

4x

2x

2x

3x

2x

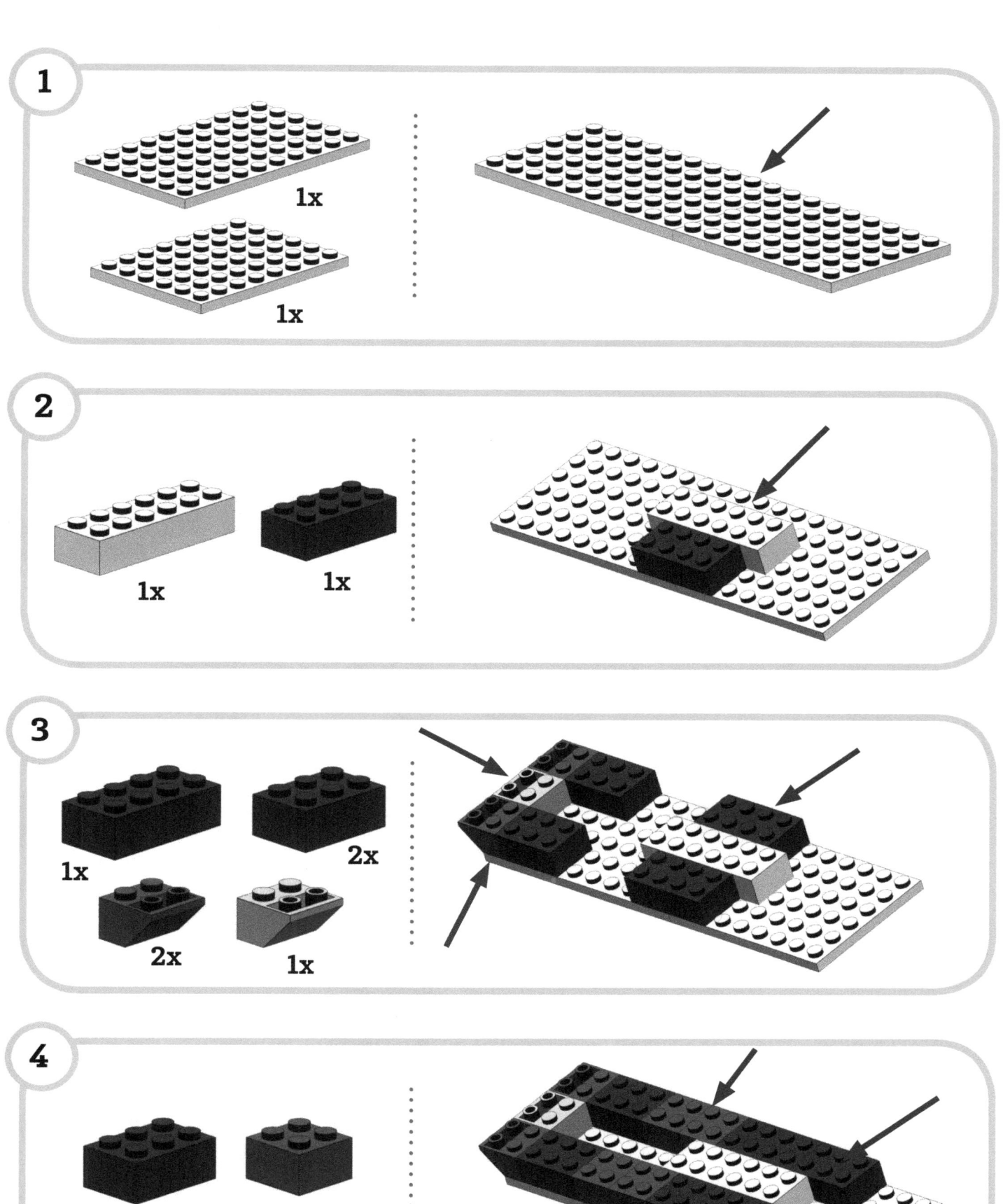

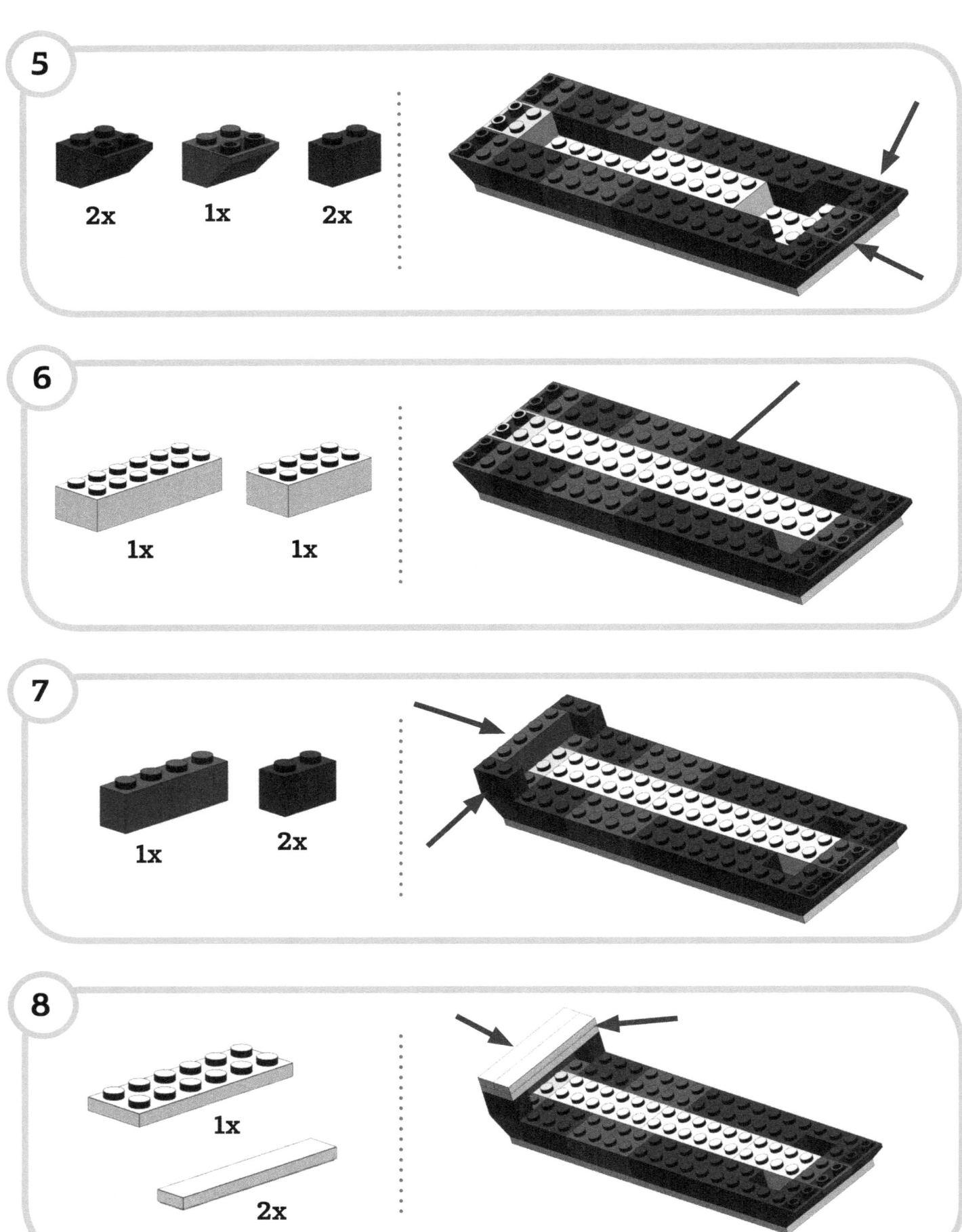

70

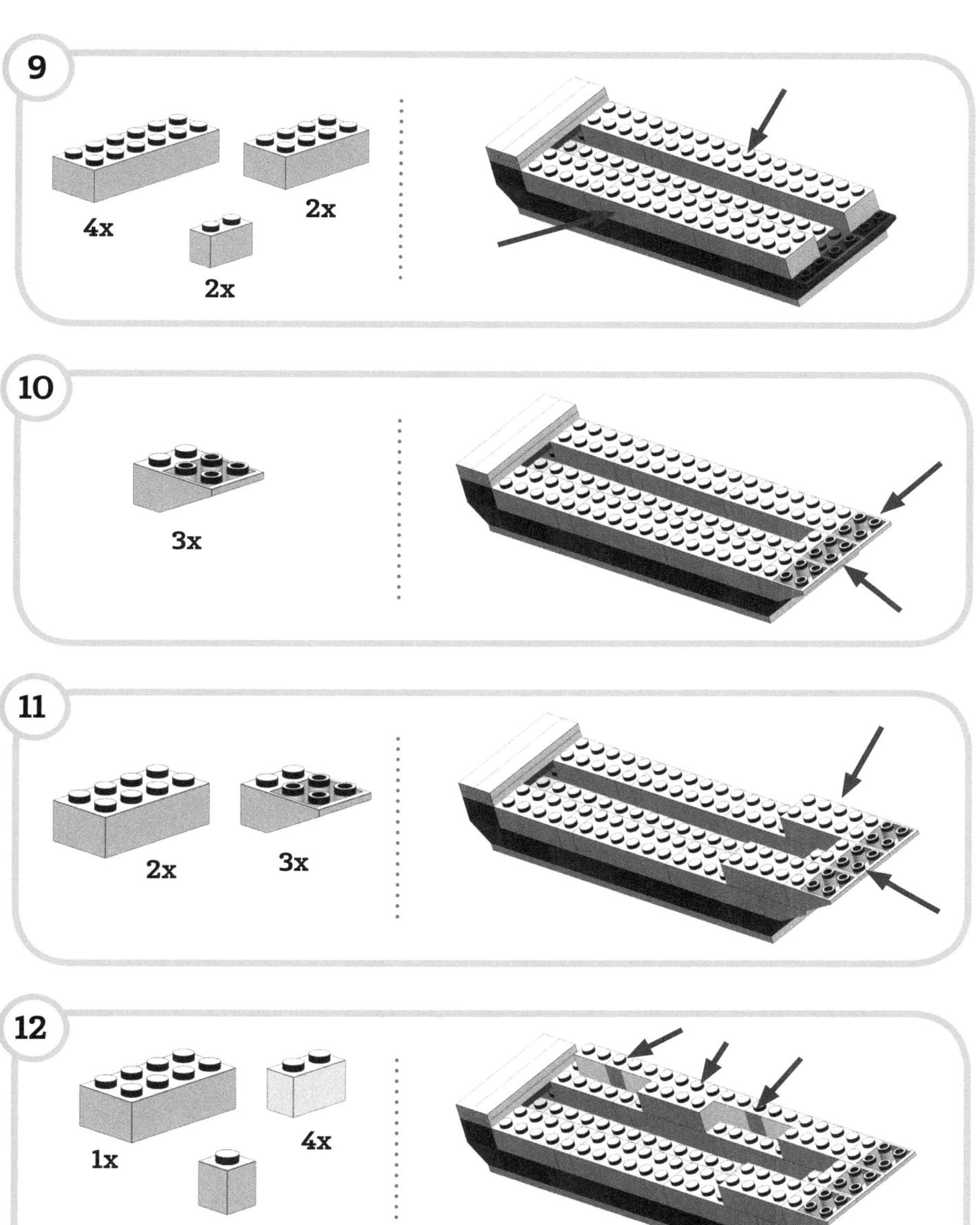

71

13

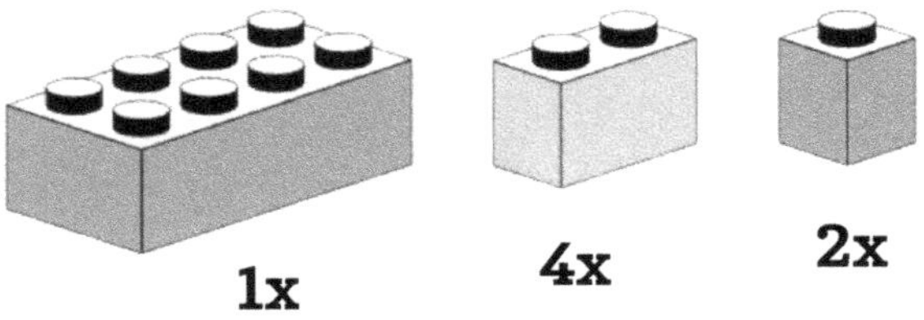

1x

4x

2x

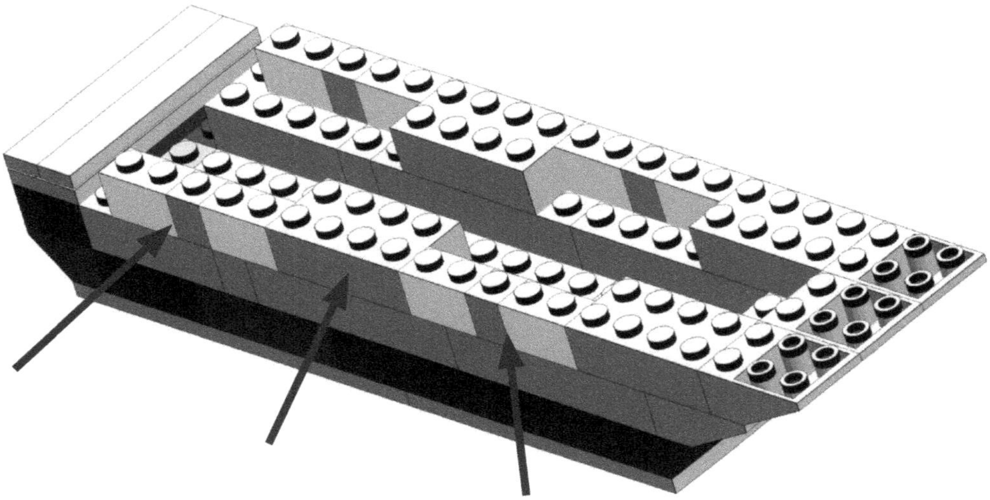

14

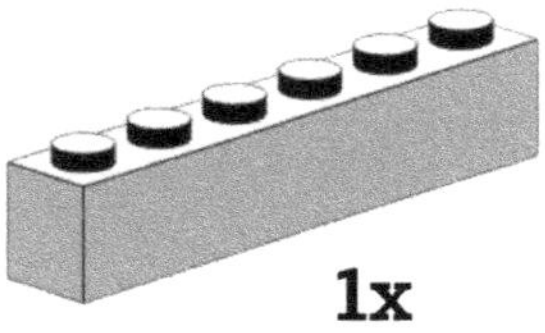

1x

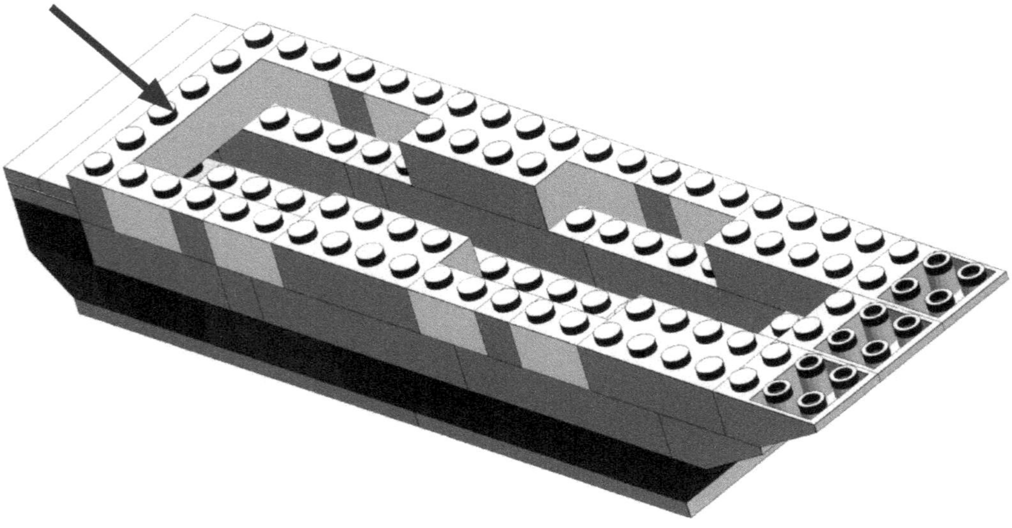

15

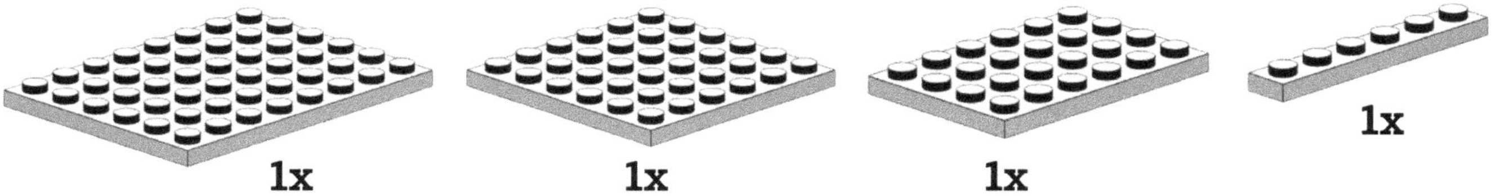

1x   1x   1x   1x

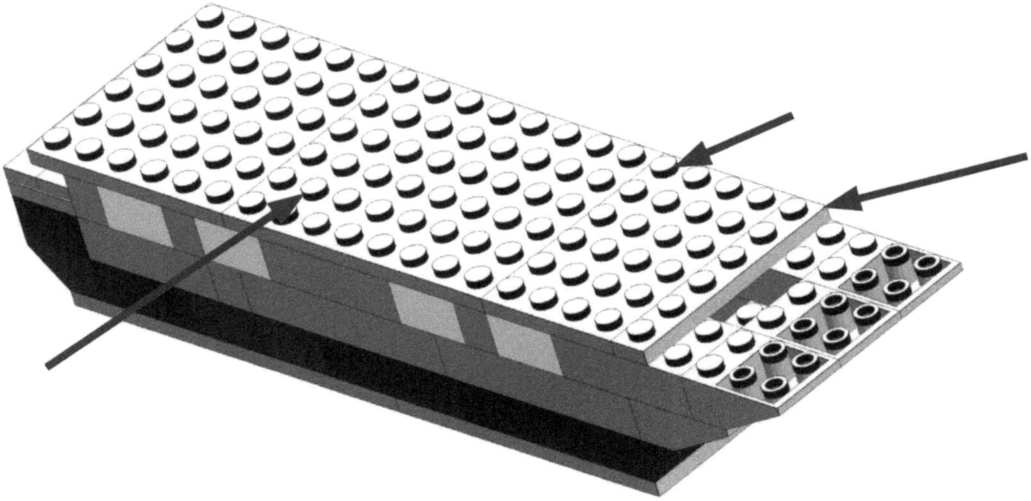

16

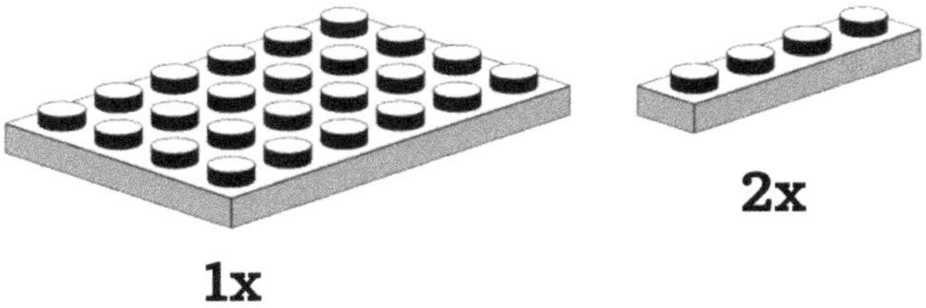

1x   2x

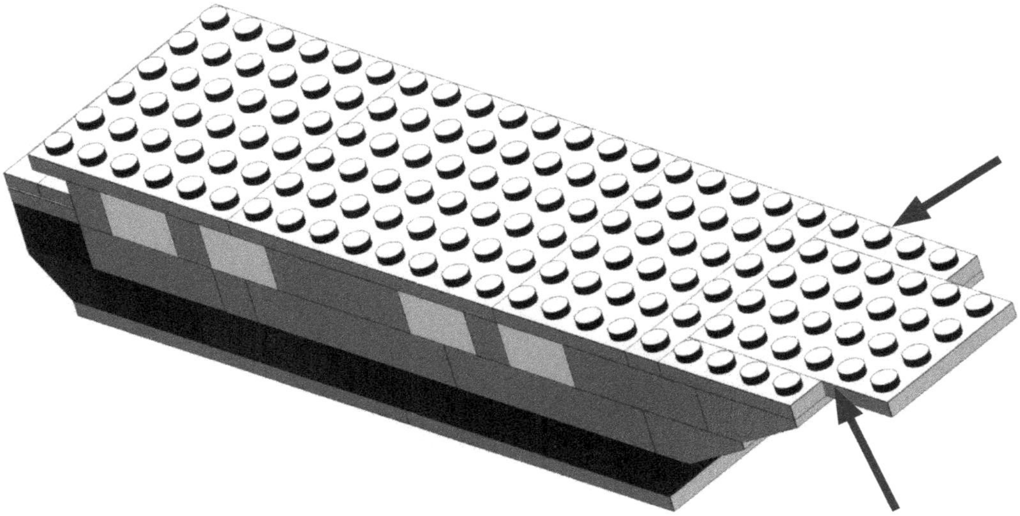

17

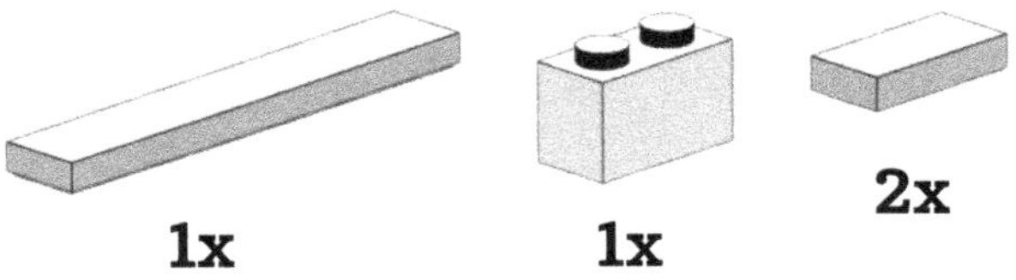

1x 1x 2x

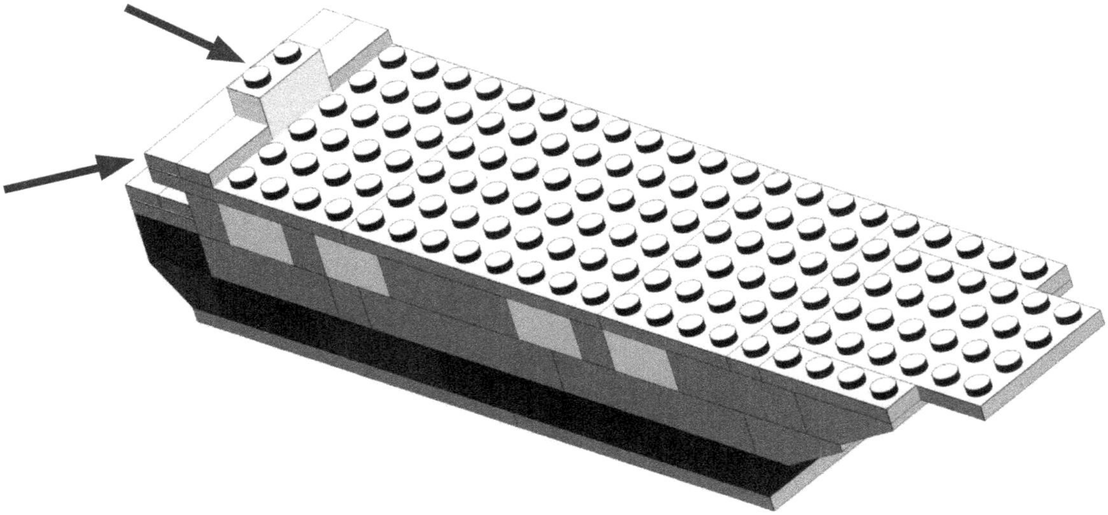

18

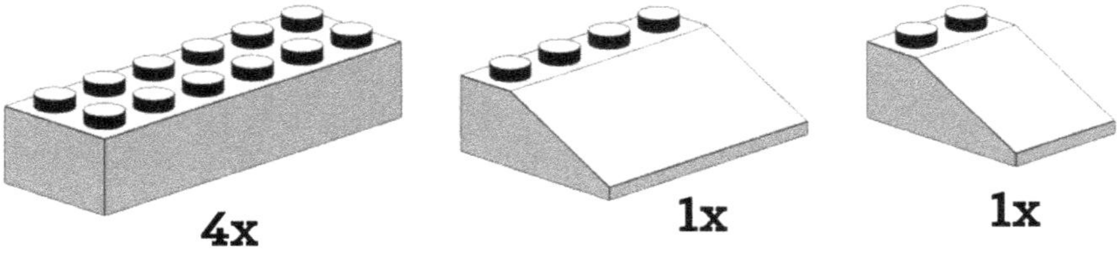

4x 1x 1x

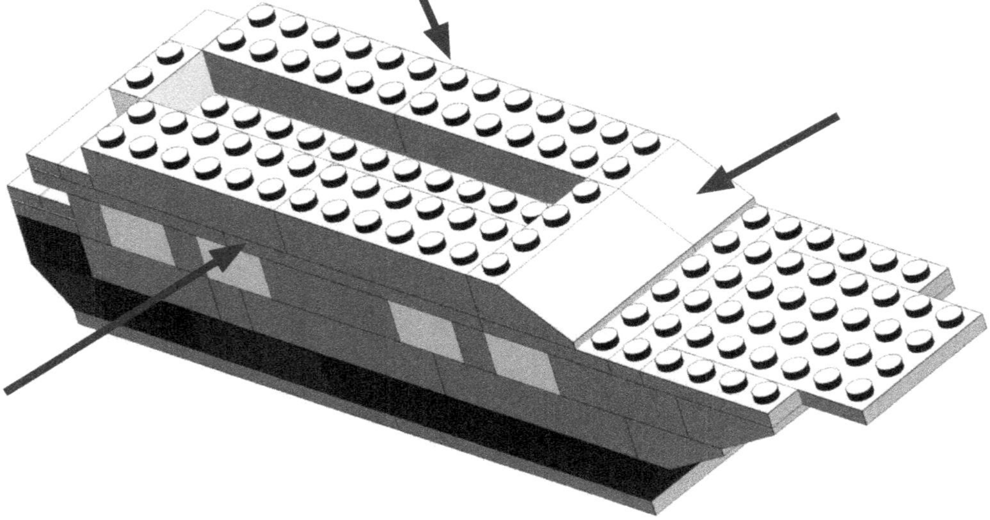

19

4x **2x**

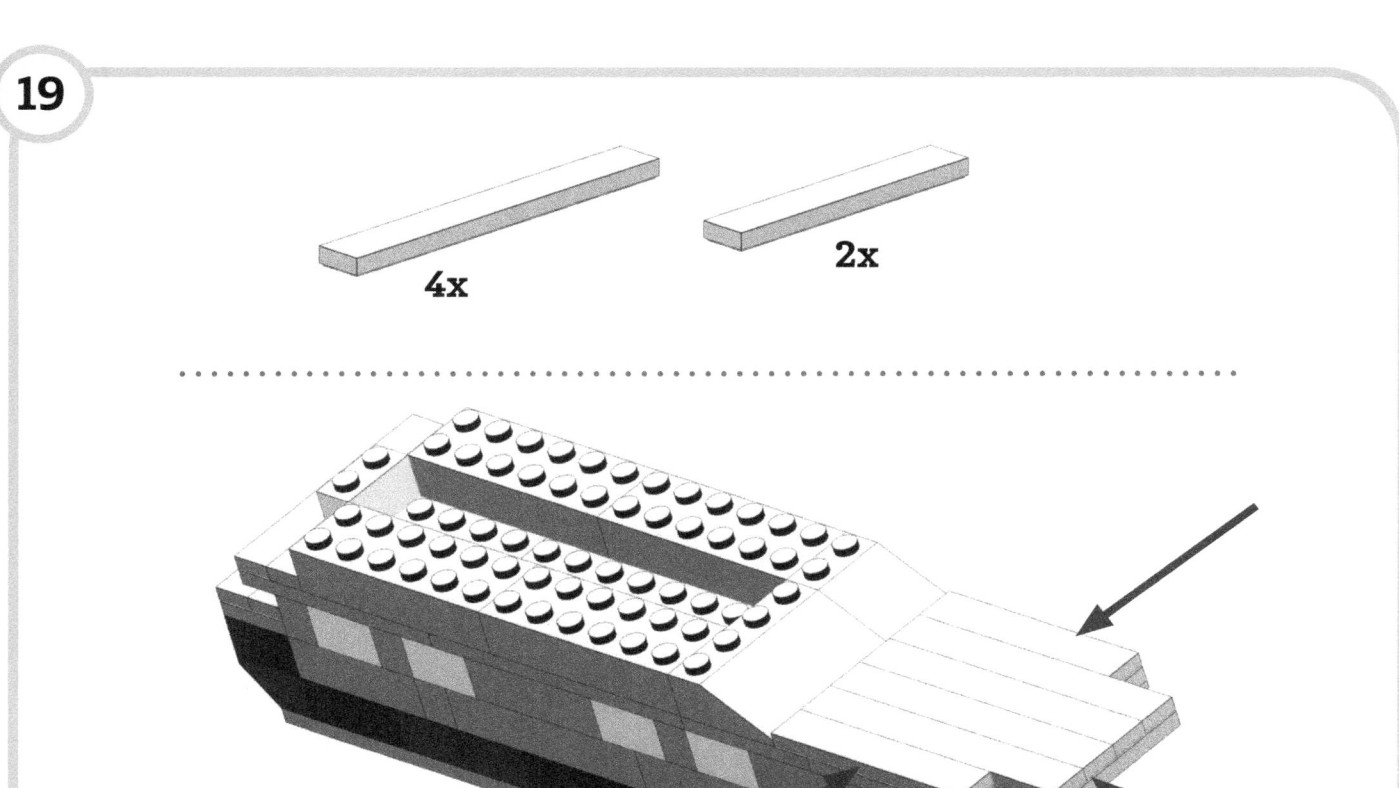

20

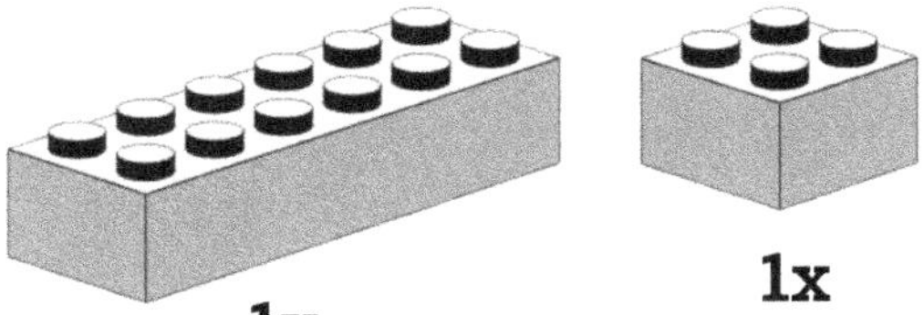

1x **1x**

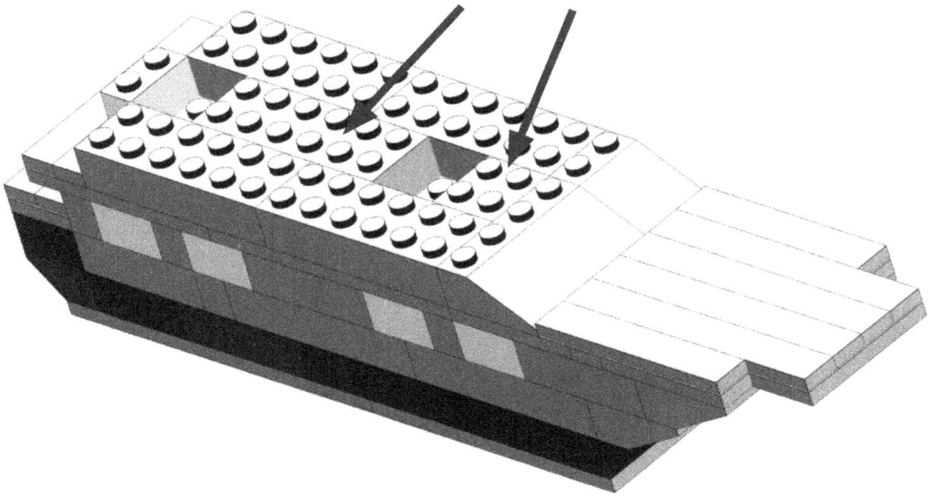

21

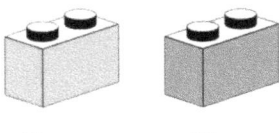

3x   2x

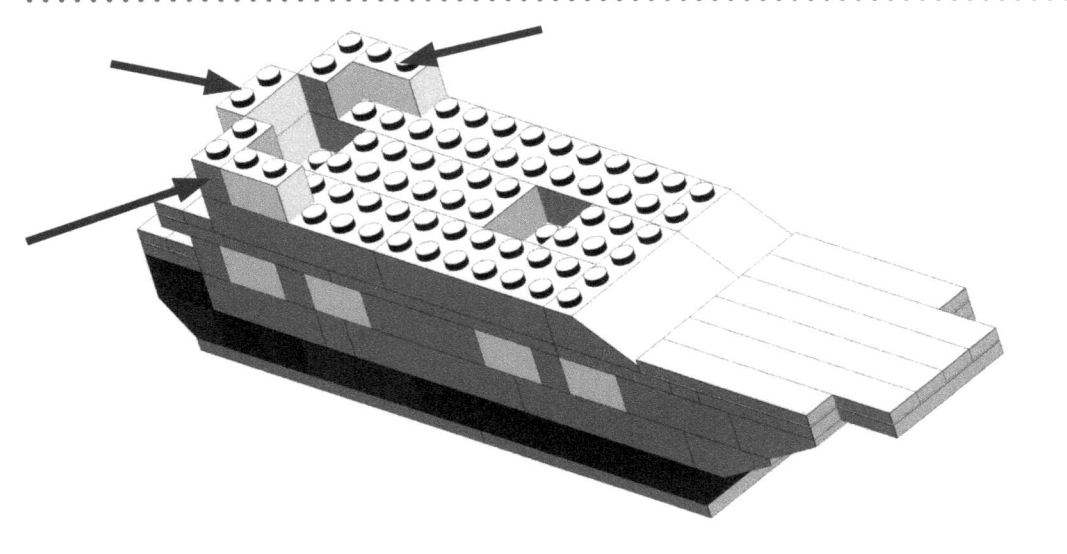

22

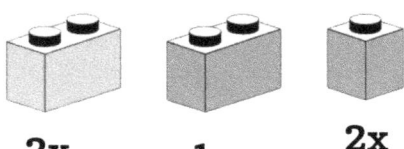

2x   1x   2x

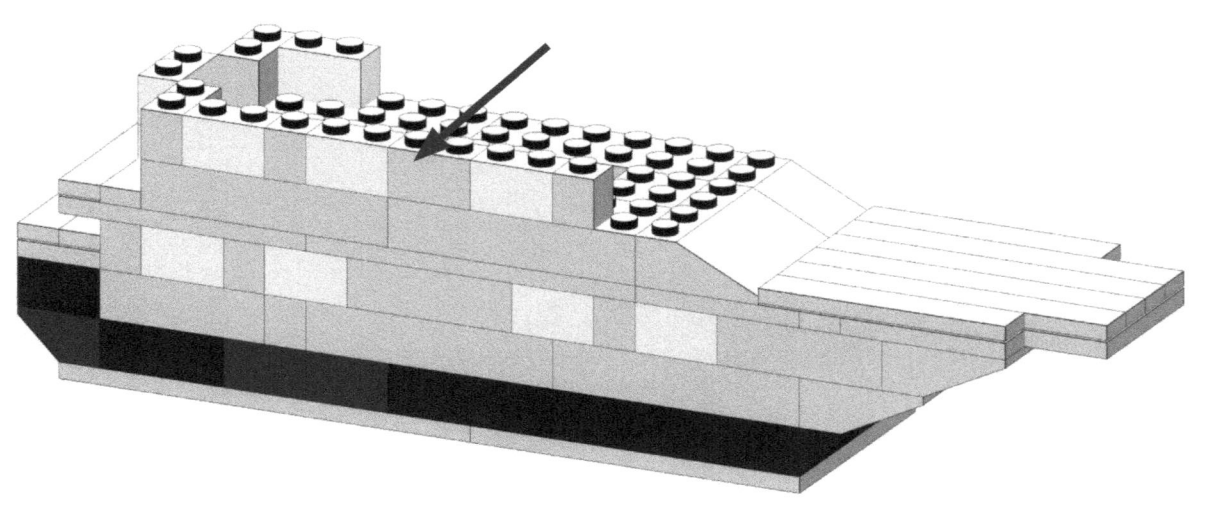

23

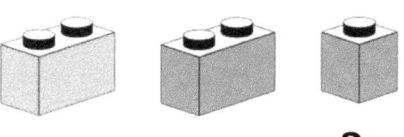

2x   1x   2x

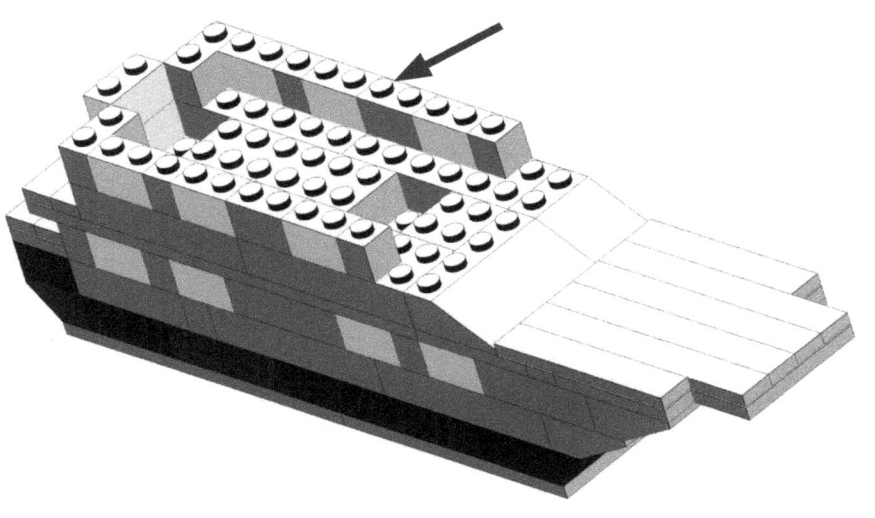

24

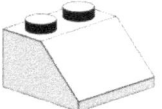

3x

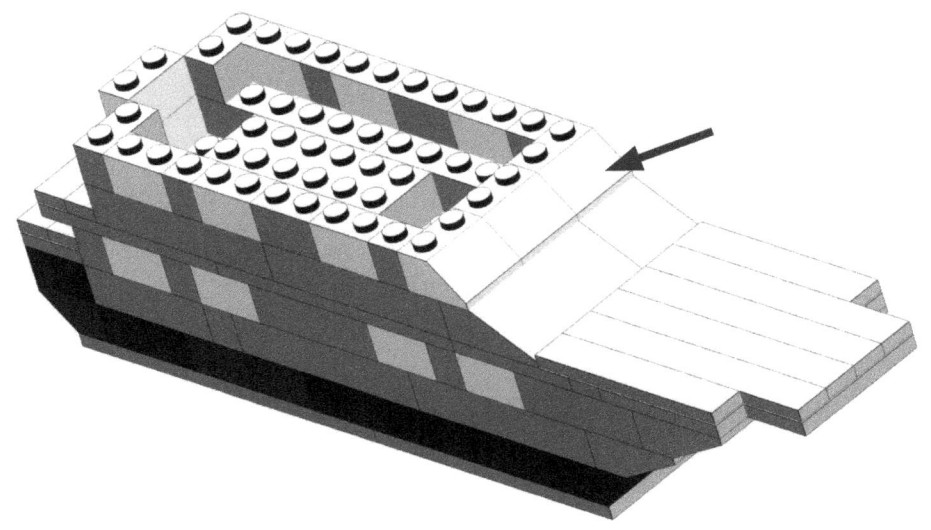

25

1x

1x

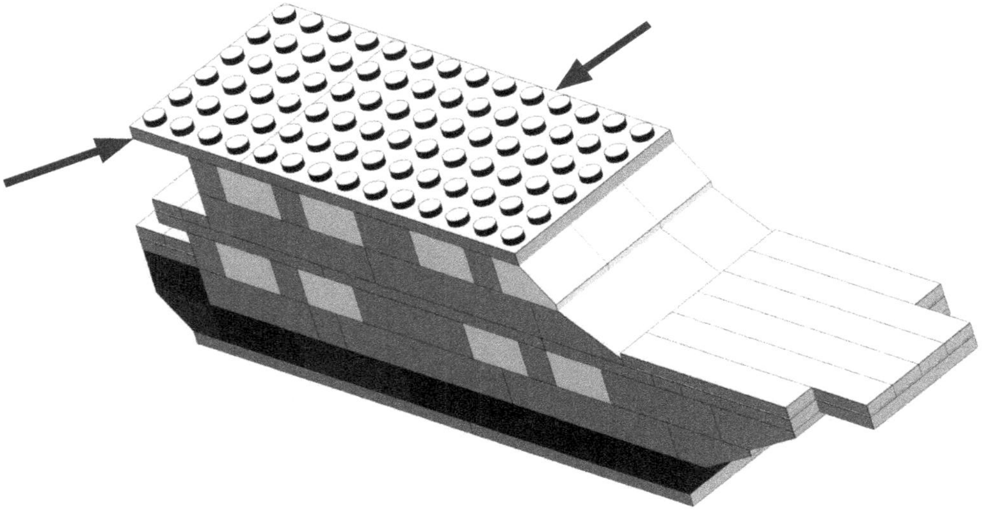

26

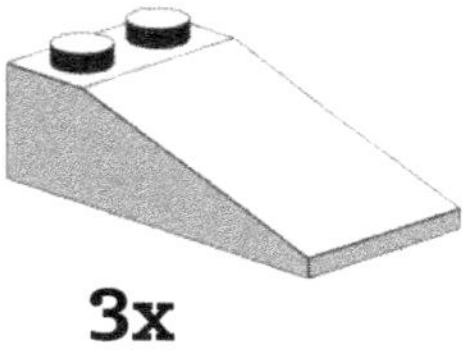

3x

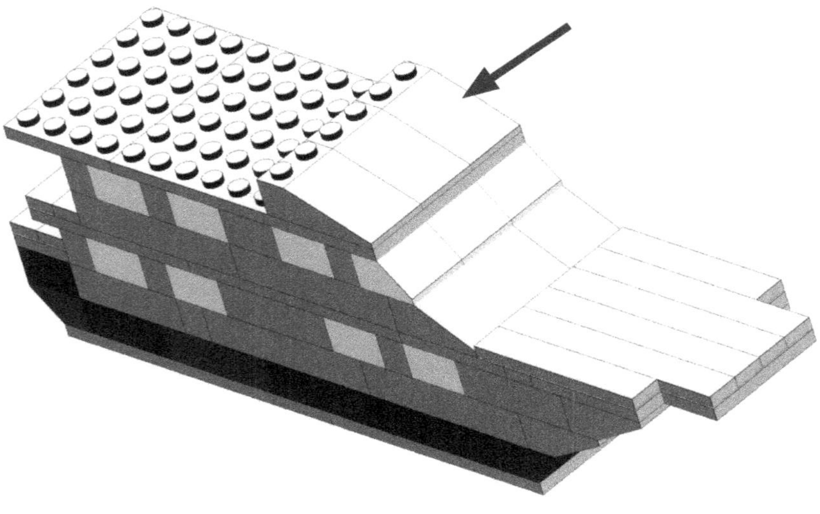

3x

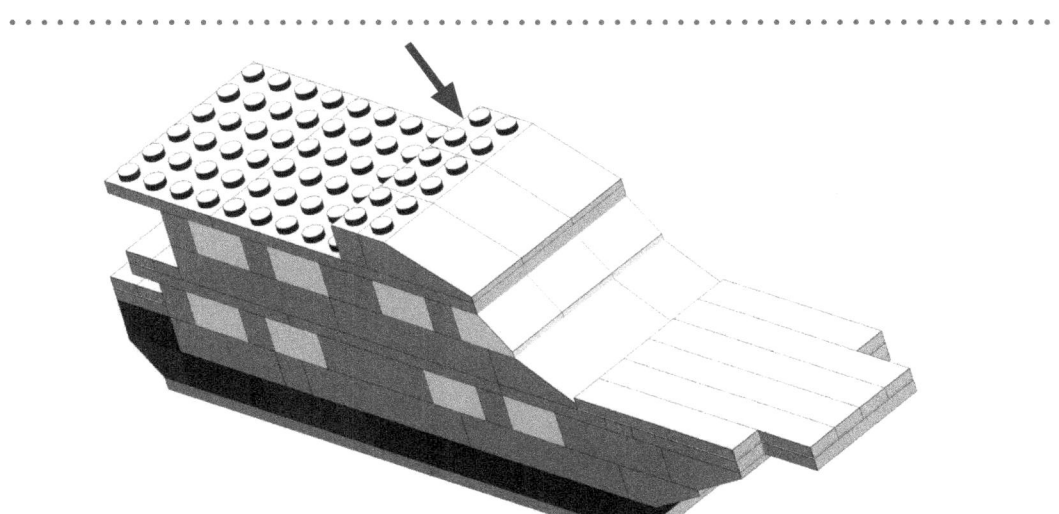

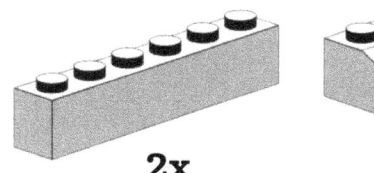

28

2x   3x

29

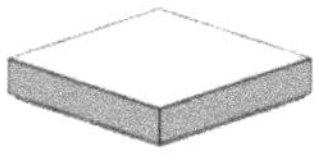

3x

1x

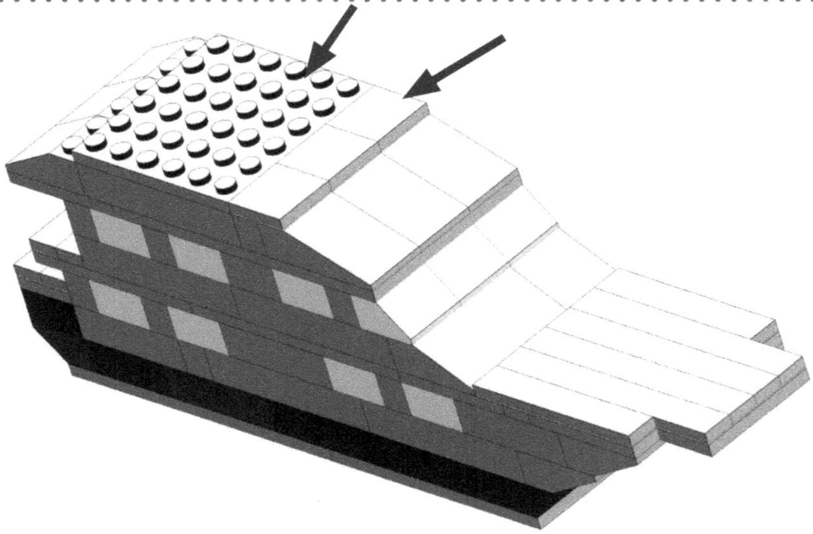

30

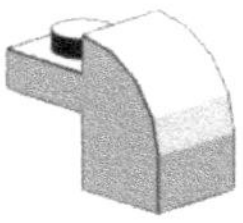

2x

1x

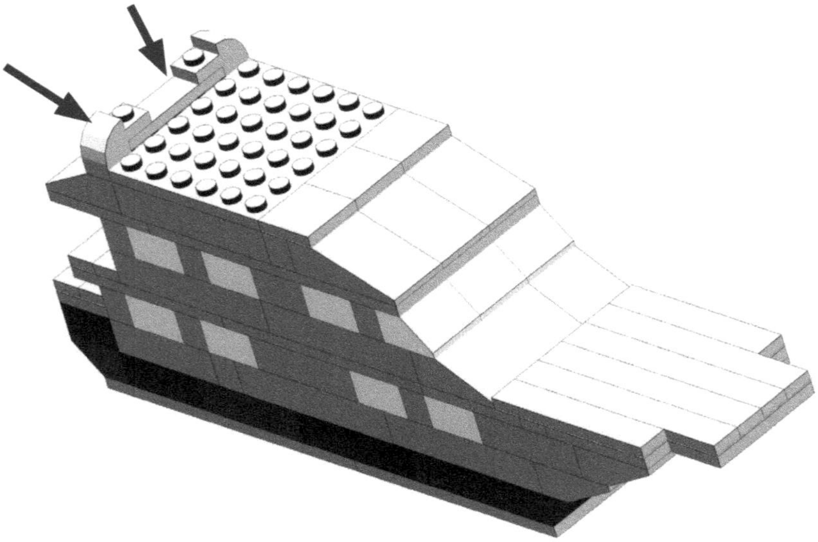

31

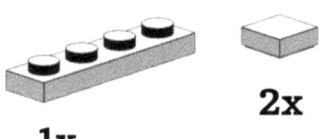

1x 2x

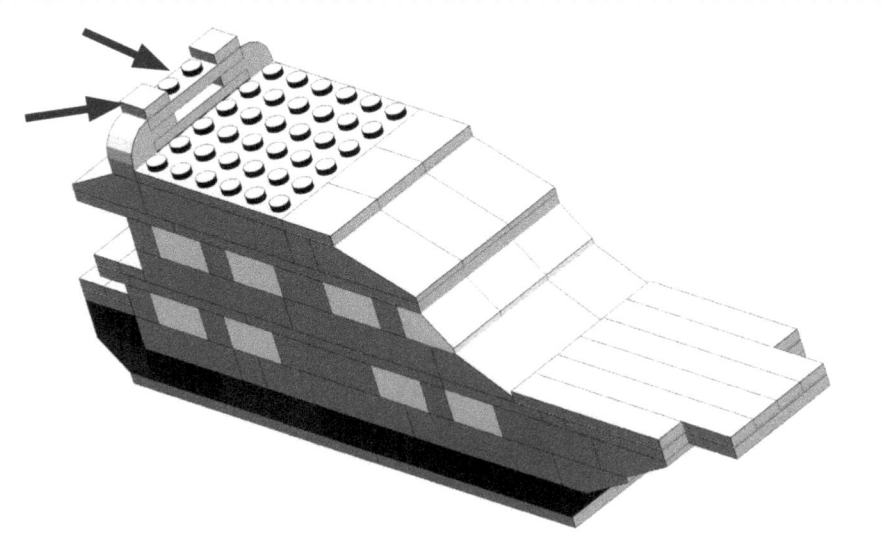

32

2x 2x 2x 2x 2x

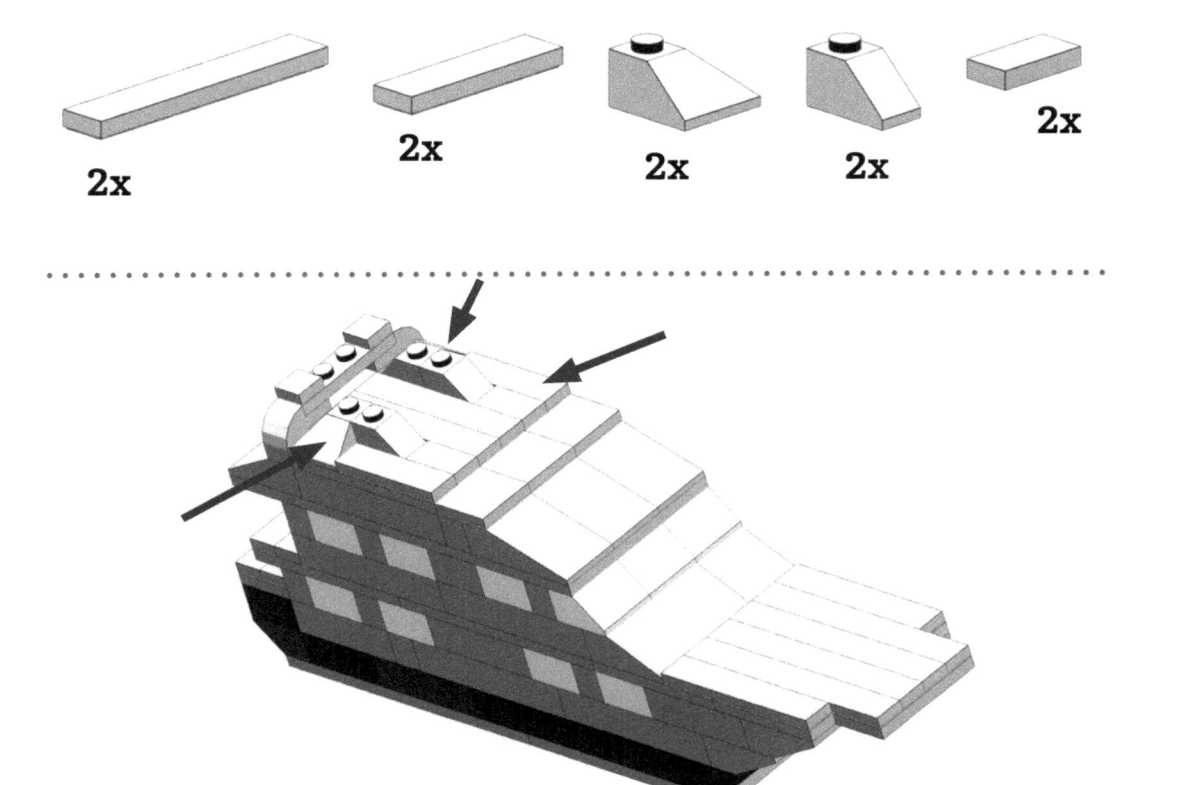

1x

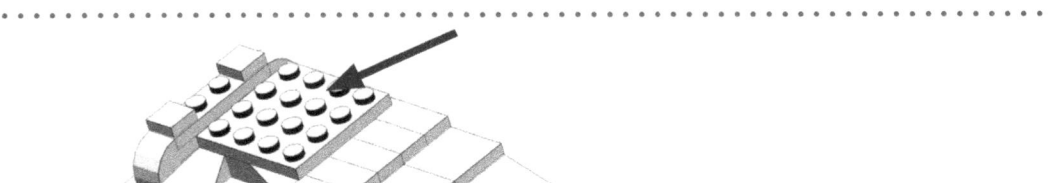

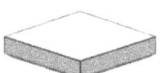

4x

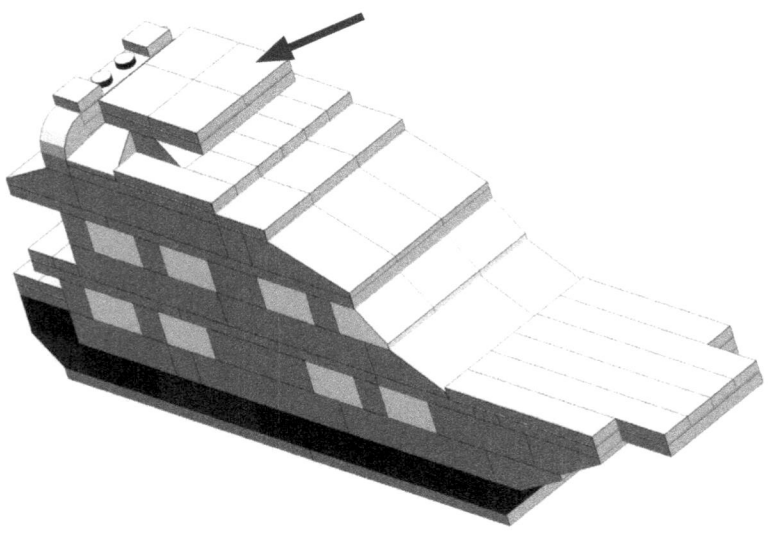

35

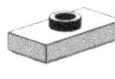
1x

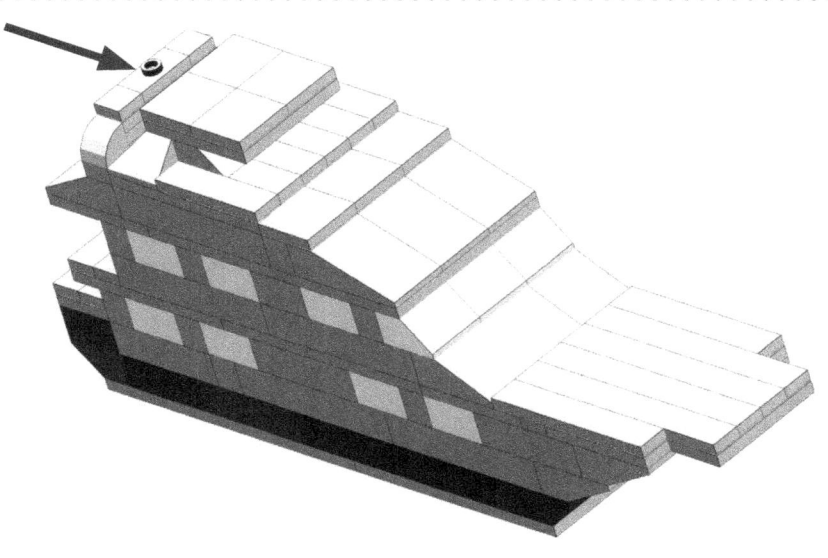

36

2x 1x

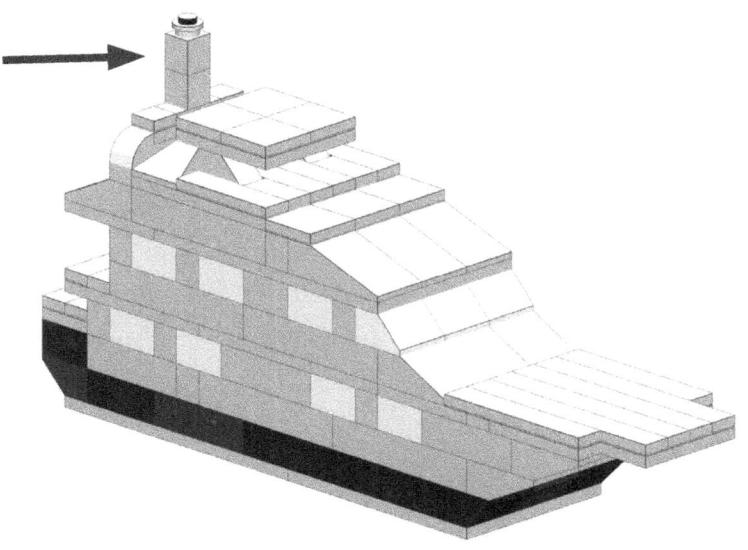

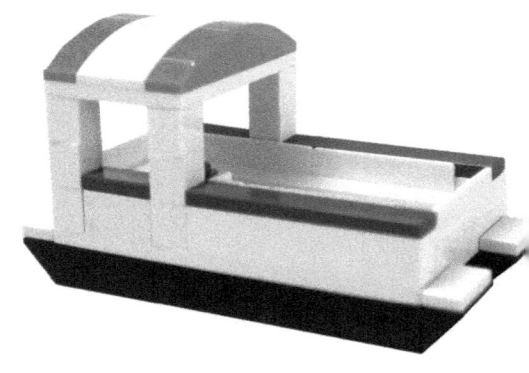

Library of Congress Control Number: 2016918964
International Standard Book Number: 978-1-513260-55-6 (paperback)
978-1-513260-57-0 (hardbound) | 978-1-513260-56-3 (e-book)

Designer: Vicki Knapton

Graphic Arts Books
An imprint of

GRAPHIC ARTS
BOOKS®

GraphicArtsBooks.com

Proudly distributed by Ingram Publisher Services.

The following artists hold copyright to their images as indicated:
Sailboats on front cover (bottom), pages 6-7: Reljic Aleksandra/Shutterstock.com;
Sports Boats on front cover (middle), pages 28-29: alexmstudio/Shutterstock.com;
Boat-a-palooza on pages 1, 42-43, back cover: iStock.com/denisik11.

The author thanks the LDraw community for the parts database it makes available, which is used for making instructions found in the book. For more information on LDraw, please visit ldraw.org.

Make sure your **Build It!** library is complete

○ Volume 1

○ Volume 2

○ Volume 3

○ World Landmarks

○ Things that Fly

○ Things that Go

○ Things that Float

○ Robots

○ Farm Animals

○ Dinosaurs

○ Trains

○ Sea Life

Visit GraphicArtsBooks.com for more titles in the series